# Profit is Not a
# Four Letter Word

## A Guide for Small Business Owners

### Sherri Gallagher

Pas Auf Publishing

# Contents

# Acknowledgements

The photo on page 85 courtesy of Robert C. Spaid and rights owned by the author. All other photos, images, and graphs were selected from https://pixabay.com and were listed as free for commercial use.

The quotes from W. Edwards Deming were retrieved from https:// wikipedia.org and are footnoted accordingly.

Charts in Chapter 11, Anchors Away, are annotated as to their source and represent the most current data available from the Bureau of Labor and Statistics at the time of printing.

Thank you to Jane Steen, Judy Knox, and Cathy Harvey for reading and editing a non-fiction work.

Thank you to "genophile" (fiverr.com/genophile) for designing the cover.

Thank you to Steven Booth for formatting.

# Introduction

In today's challenging economic environment, small business owners are getting squeezed by both their bigger competitors and the government. Big businesses can afford to ship their money to foreign countries to avoid taxes and retain profits, but that strategy is seldom available to the small company. And yet, small businesses employ 53% of the workforce.

A small business owner who wants to create jobs, earn an income for their family, create a stable and safe place to work for their employees, and save up a nest-egg for retirement is being driven out of business by eroding profits and competition from bigger companies. What can be done?

*Profit is Not a Four Letter Word* is a no-nonsense guide to help the small business owner decide where to spend to get the best long-term return. It is for the person who actively oversees all elements of the business. It is not for those who want to get in, make a quick big buck, and get out.

The engine for growth in the United States is the small company, defined as having under $50 million in sales and generally less than 100 employees. These are the people I have worked with for over 35 years. My goal has been to help each of them implement the best system for their individual needs. No two companies I have worked with have had the same needs, so no two systems we have developed together have been the same.

For a very long time I have been called in to rescue companies who were "up the unsanitary tributary without a visible means of locomotion." (Feel free to translate that into more common vernacular.) More recently I have worked with companies interested in getting independent certifications. I have also seen an increasing demand for trained individuals to create labor standards and even economic order quantities. I help these clients by using my education and experience in business over the last three decades, and my ability to troubleshoot and solve problems. Hopefully this book will help you get a little closer to the answers you need for your business to grow and thrive.

Please feel free to implement the things that make the most sense for your company and ignore the rest. No two companies have the same needs so not everything will apply to your situation. Use your best judgment and do what's best for your company. If you want to contact me you can find me at technacon1986@ sbcglobal.net or at www.technacon.com.

—Sherri Gallagher

# Chapter 1

Fly Poop in the Pepper

**Chapter in a Nutshell:**
Don't waste resources on an unnecessary level of detail, save it for the analysis where it will make a difference.

At times I will suggest reports and data analysis to help you, the business owner, with the decisions you have to make. Much of the data collection can be delegated to your staff. When you do the delegation, make sure the staff are not trying to pick the fly poop out of the pepper. In other words, use a level of accuracy necessary to get the job done and nothing more. Don't waste resources getting the big picture defined beyond a level needed to make an educated decision.

Chances are, you are working at the macro level, and the micro level comes later. Most companies have more projects than they have resources, which can be a major problem and can lead to overextension and sometimes even the collapse of the business. Therefore, you are looking to do corporate **triage** to make sure you can stay on track. You need to look for enough information to deploy those scarce resources.

> **Triage** is a term often used in the medical profession to sort mass casualties. They are looking to separate minor injuries from serious injuries. Who can wait and who needs help immediately? It occurs when the need exceeds the resources.

Ask yourself:

- Which project is going to drive the most profit to the bottom line or create the biggest increase in revenue/sales or minimize the corporate risk?
- How much of the company's resources will each project consume?
- How long will it take to complete the project? A day? A week? A year? A decade?

Don't overwhelm your staff with demands for precision. Make sure they understand you want them to look at the big picture. No one's continued employment should rest on being accurate to the hundredth of a penny. If a staffer needs a month and three engineers to get you the data they are probably looking at too detailed a level or, to use the analogy above, they are looking for fly poop in the pepper.

## Real life example

My son is a mechanical engineer. He was tasked to design railings for a catwalk in a plant. The directive was to make the drawings with a +/- .005 inch tolerance. He laughed his rear end off since he understood the guys building the railings were working with tape measures not micrometers. The guys building the railings would be doing an outstanding job if their accuracy was +/- .125 inches.

## Needed Information

Projects have three components to weigh:

- Time
- Scope
- Resources

**Time:** How long will this project take to complete? A project may have a medium return on investment but it can be turned around quickly versus another project that will have a huge impact on the bottom line but will take multiple sales cycles to implement. Only you know your situation. Sometimes spending more can reduce the time to accomplish the project, sometimes it won't.

Different companies have different sales cycles. A company manufacturing cookies or candy has a much shorter sales cycle than a company building CNC machines. To the food company a week is a tremendously long time but to the CNC builder it is a small fraction of the sales cycle. A project taking a week will have very different meanings to each of the companies. It is a matter of perspective and must be looked at from the perspective of your company.

**Scope:** Does everyone understand what is and is not included in the project? It is important to define the project clearly so it doesn't migrate. You are applying limited resources. Everyone on the project team must agree on what the project will and won't accomplish or your resource estimates could be in error and the project may take more time and/or cost more.

**Resources:** There are more costs than just the capital investment. Most companies don't have full time staff sitting around doing nothing who can be allocated to a new project at the drop of a hat. Project resources are going to be taken away from day to day operations. It could be people, equipment, software, tribal knowledge[1] or innovation skills. While you want to focus on the big picture, you need to know what the impact is on day-to-day operations and future product launches.

## Data Accuracy

It is okay to use estimates to get an order of magnitude on a problem. If you are logging non-conformances into a Cost of Quality report on the first pass, don't worry about collecting every last minute of time spent resolving issues. To start, get an educated estimate. You may end up assigning a half hour of clerical labor and one hour of engineering labor to each non-conformance. Is it an accurate number? Of course not, but it should be a representative cost that allows you to compare what is spent on inspection/prevention versus where the system fails and determine where to apply resources to get the most improvement.

---

1 Tribal knowledge is defined as information pertinent to your specific company only learned through experience or taught by more experienced employees

Look at the stone wall in the picture. Think of each stone as an issue preventing you from achieving greater profits. Which stone are you going to remove from the wall first so you can get to those profits? The biggest one, right? Apply the same logic to gathering your data and go after the big things that will have the most impact first.

## Digging Down

Once you have decided on a situation to address, then it's time to improve the accuracy of the data. Using the example of the non-conformance again, where we may have estimated $100/non-conformance, now we look at groupings. If one reason you identify is incorrect freight charges, we may determine it actually only costs $25 to document the issue while a non-functioning part costs $250 per issue. Sorting the data, we can again look at order of magnitude to further refine where we apply scarce resources. If we have twenty incorrect freight issues versus one non-functioning part, we may decide to attack the freight billing problem first since it is costing you twice as much. This is especially important because, in addition to the in-house cost, there are 20 dissatisfied customers. On the other hand, the non-functioning part may open us to a huge liability suit and take fewer resources as well. In that case resources may be better assigned to the non-functioning part even though the cost is lower and affects fewer customers. The potential cost of liability and litigation should be considered, even if they are speculative.

The point is always to apply our limited resources wisely. Don't waste a lot of time collecting data that will not help your decision-making. Instead use those resources when you need to improve the accuracy to solve the right situation.

Consider your data to be like the raw ore in the picture. If you sort on size, you can decide which has the greatest value. Is the loose powder an immediate salable product? Your error in freight charges may be like the loose powder, quick and easy profits to add to the bottom line. Consider the big chunks of ore like the non-functioning product. Deal with one and the biggest cost goes away. Only you can know which is the best application in your particular business. Once you make the decision and apply resources, stick with it until you fix the problem. I will talk about a few common tools to perform the analysis in the chapter titled, "Alligator Alley."

## When to Measure

If you are going to have people spend time taking a measurement, then it is worth taking the time to record the measurement. If resources have been spent recording measurements, then it is worth analyzing the data. If it is worth analyzing the data, then it is worth taking action. If there is no point in taking action, then we shouldn't have taken the measurement in the first place.

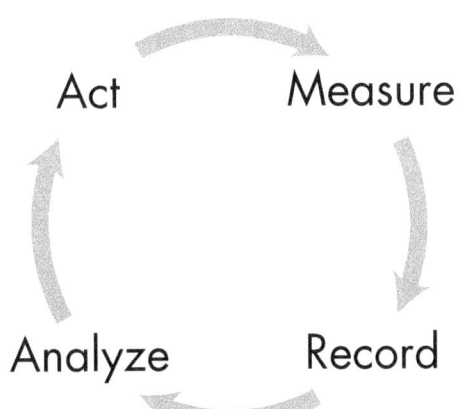

If you follow Deming, then you may notice a similarity to his Plan-Do-Check-Act cycle. Continuous improvement is cyclical in nature and is very dependent on data. Deming was a statistician who was very aggressive in making sure data was used correctly.

## Real life example

I visited a client who had a very upset customer. My client made mating plastic thermoform parts at two different plants. The parts pressed together using an interference fit. The problem was, the parts didn't always match up. Sometimes they couldn't be pressed together. Sometimes they wouldn't stay together. I was tasked with "fix it before we lose our customers." Management at each plant was very upset. I was told I needed to understand that the operators were overworked and if I wanted any additional tests added to their workload, it would cause a serious problem. I observed employees taking extensive measurements with a caliper and carefully noting the results. None of the measurements related to the interference surfaces. When I asked how the data was used, the plant management gave me blank stares. They were unaware that measurements were being taken. When I asked the employees why they were taking the measurements they said they had been directed by the toolmaker to take them. This was a problem because the toolmaker had retired two years earlier. When we contacted him, we found out that he modified the tool two years before he left and had needed some quick data to verify the tool was functioning as expected. He had wanted two shifts of data and nothing more. The employees had collected data for four years for no reason at all. We stopped the caliper measurements, built some quick fixtures to test the interference fit which reduced the operator workload, and solved the end customer's problem.

### Real life example

Another company brought me in because their customer was receiving non-conforming parts frequently. The customer insisted they implement 100% inspection until the problem was resolved. My client was collecting statistical data on a key characteristic. It was clear on the charts when the process was out of control. I asked the operator what they were supposed to do when the screen turned red (the program's method of indicating an out of control condition). The operator told me she didn't know she was supposed to do anything. She entered data and went back to work. That was her job. I quizzed the engineers and managers, asking who reviewed the statistical data. They had downsized and the engineer who had implemented the Statistical Process Control (SPC) had been let go. Since he left, no one had the time or the responsibility to look at the charts. The out of control condition had a direct relationship to the non-conformance their customer was reporting. Using a little training and a little documentation we solved the problem.

In the first example unnecessary measurements were being taken. They had no value to the company or the end customer and almost prevented the implementation of actions which added value to the process. In the second example, the data was not being analyzed or addressed. In both cases resources were being wasted. Of course, the second problem had some serious communication issue components, but that is topic of the next chapter, "I Said."

## Pareto Principle

Dr. Joseph Juran applied a 19th century philosopher's concept to quality issues. As business people have now learned it applies in most applications. The concept known as the Pareto Principle says 20% of your products will constitute 80% of sales. Similarly, 20% of your products will produce 80% of the non-conformances. Because limited resources are involved, make sure they are applied to the "vital few" 20% and not the "trivial many" 80%.

## Summary

- Don't waste resources with unnecessary levels of accuracy.
- Don't spend more on data collection than you can get back in savings and eliminated risk.
- Use order of magnitude to determine the level of accuracy you really need.
- Measure only what you need to get results.
- If you collect data use it, or lose it and save the resources for something you will act on.

# Chapter 2

I Said …

**Chapter in a Nutshell:**
Clear communication is key to moving waste from the scrap bin to the bottom line. Just keep it simple.

In the first chapter, one of my clients had a serious communication problem. A toolmaker wanted specific data collected for a couple of shifts to verify changes in a tool. The operators continued to collect data for four years. How did this happen? Poor communication. No one told the operators why the data was being collected. The assumption was they didn't need to know. Without complete information resources were wasted.

**Real life example**

A medical device company manufactured and plated its own products. They had a reputation for high quality and durable products. Plating was key to the life of the product. Twelve operators spent their day inspecting the plating. The inspectors took their job seriously. As they looked at the plated parts, they noticed small nuances. At one point they identified what they thought were swirls in the knurling and rejected hundreds of parts. The swirls were only visible if held a specific way in specific lighting and had nothing to do with the function or perceived aesthetics of the part. The engineering staff did a lot of work setting up examples of good and non-conforming parts to help the inspectors, but hundreds of parts continued to be rejected, each time for a new perceived non-conformance. We took the lead inspectors out on a couple of sales calls and asked them to listen to the interaction with the customers and what was important to the customer. We then held discussion sessions with all the inspectors. Once they understood what the customer was really looking for in the product the rejections went down to almost zero. Any new rejections related to the function or end customer perception.

In both cases the people making the product were given incomplete information. Business owners need to address the assumptions and incomplete communication to prevent this kind of wasted resources. It sounds simple but poor communication is one of the most common sources of failure. Contracts, sales orders, and purchase orders are key methods of communication. Make sure they communicate the end user's needs. Drawings and specifications tell the people making the product what is and isn't important.

### Real life example

I had just started working for an automotive supplier as the chief quality officer. My third day on the job I got a call from a very irate first tier automaker telling me our parts were junk. Again. The threats and demands were significant. I followed up, pulled parts from stock and had them measured. They were well within specification to our in-house print. I checked our SPC data, first and last piece inspections, but everything pointed to the parts being to print. The roll form where they were made was checked and didn't have any maintenance issues. It didn't make sense. I started working backwards. If the parts and tooling were correct to the print where did we get the print information? Comparing our print to the customer print sent on the original quotation, I found a key angle had been transposed in the transfer to our prints. In essence we were making the parts backwards.

The point where communication usually fails is in the hand off. What are the difficulties your sales staff experience when passing on information? If this hand off fails nothing the rest of the employees do, no matter how dedicated and careful, is going to do anything other than waste resources.

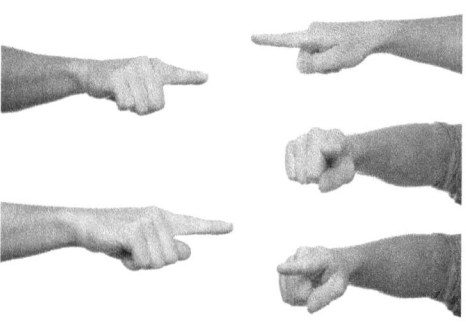

Also consider how well do the engineers and designers pass on the information to the toolmakers and the production staff. In the example above, this was a real oops. The funny part of that one was that some of the operators were really into cars, and therefore were familiar with how this part was used. We generated temporary tooling to get the parts to the automaker while the permanent tool was manufactured. As soon as we explained how the part was used, the operators knew exactly what had happened. They did an excellent job of testing and tracking our production until the permanent fix was in place. Who knows, if we had told them how the part was being used in the first place, they might have spotted the mistake at the start up.

In today's manufacturing, communication doesn't stop with the operators. Shipping and logistics are now a very big piece of the pie. Customers are using returnable containers and pallets. They have specific shipping methods and delivery requirements. How does this information get passed on to the guy calling in the freight hauler?

## Keep It Simple Sweetheart (KISS)

The balancing act with communication is getting the right data to the right people and nothing more. Having sales or any employee complete long detailed forms is just as problematic as going free-form and allowing any type of communication. If the information can't fit on one page be very suspicious. Unless your product is a commodity with no special handling or instructions required, question any system that does not allow for special needs and instructions.

**Real life example**

A client brought me in to look at their Quality Management System (QMS). Starting at the beginning I asked management how the outside sales communicated with the inside sales. I was shown a very detailed form the sales staff completed and forwarded to order entry. It was impressive. Order entry came next. I asked how they received the sales rep's forms and they laughed. None of the sales staff used the form. Inside sales pieced things together from e-mails, previous orders, and phone calls. Going back to sales, we asked why they didn't use the form. They answered that it was too detailed, much of the information was not needed, and it was very difficult to open, save, and send. An e-mail was quicker and easier for the sales reps so they could get back out selling. A redesign of the form set up in a standard e-mail solved the problem. Order entry no longer needed overtime to get the job done, nor to chase down information and disrupt production for an in-house rush job.

## Going Back the Other Way

Communication isn't a one-way street. It doesn't just flow from the customer through the system and out from shipping. It is not just rolling the rocks downhill. This is an old concept but worth repeating, the next person to use your output is your customer. So order entry is the customer of the sales rep. Engineering is the customer of order entry and the sales staff. Tooling is the customer of engineering. Production is the customer of engineering and tooling. Shipping is the customer of manufacturing and order entry. The end user is the customer of shipping. Sales is the customer of the customer.

Order entry and engineering have to communicate back to the sales reps. They have to be able to say, "Your mouth is writing a ticket our rear-ends have to pay. I need…." Shipping has to be able to communicate what information they need and in what time frame to perform their job correctly.

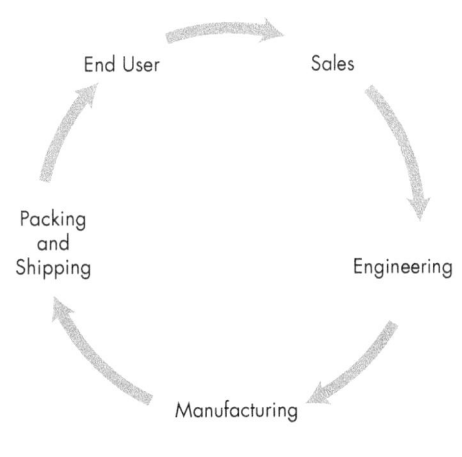

### Real life example

I met with a new client who wanted to revise their ISO 9001 system. To get a feel for the process I started at order entry and asked them to pull out current open orders. I picked three at random and headed for engineering. The very first one had a revision issue. The customer was ordering to a revision that required new tooling. Engineering sent an e-mail to order entry telling them the product could not be produced. The rep answered just send the old revision stuff and process the order; they'll never know. Sales confirmed the order with the customer along with a delivery to the new revision. Engineering refused to approve the release of the production order without the proper tooling. Until I started asking questions, no one realized the customer was expecting parts they were not going to receive.

All of this sounds a lot like the process of defining the scope of the project, and it is. Remember: time, scope, and resources. Without a clear understanding of what is needed the amount of time to produce and the cost will skyrocket as people learn from trial and error. Blame will be passed. Only your scrap hauler will be happy and the bottom line will suffer.

## Widows and Orphans

In the example on the previous page no one felt responsible for making sure the customer was satisfied. It was the other guy's job. While that is a bit of a different problem, it does point out a scope issue in items that were not addressed, but rather assumed.  Scope responsibilities need to be assigned or people will think someone else is handling it. People need to understand exactly when their activities start and finish. The project manager needs to walk through and ask questions to make sure all responsibilities are assigned. Here is another old chestnut: assume makes an ass out of u and me.

## Tribal Knowledge

Long-term dedicated workers are a company's most important resource. People are not a disposable commodity. Information about the special needs of your customers reside in those employees' heads and you paid for it with training or experience (e.g., through scrapped and returned product). If there is a high turnover rate in your company, you have a serious problem. Documentation may be able to prevent issues from cropping up, but lack of tribal knowledge will still create higher costs in terms of lower productivity as employees spend time referencing the documentation, asking for help, or repeating the mistakes of the past.

A long time ago, ISO 9001 documentation expected procedures to be written so the untrained individual could follow them and produce good product. Imagine the "zombie apocalypse" happened and the survivors needed your product. The idea was they could pick up your procedures and be successful at manufacturing your product. That concept was unnecessarily burdensome and, thankfully, a few iterations later, we got away from that. Your employees' knowledge is key to your success. But how do you pass on that knowledge and protect your company from being held hostage? That is addressed in the chapter titled "Gold Watch."

## Summary

- Clear communication is a key to prevention and moving dollars from the scrap containers to the bottom line.
- Contracts, purchase orders, specification sheets, and prints, when used correctly, can identify misunderstandings that must be addressed before starting, and can help prevent post-purchase dissonance.

- Project scopes must be clearly defined, including responsibilities.
- Communication requires information to flow in two directions, the next person is your customer, and you are their customer when it comes to understanding what they need.
- Information is a product.
- Keep it simple.
- Tribal knowledge is critical to your success.

# Chapter 3

Keeping Score

---

**Chapter in a Nutshell:**
Track the cost of quality
and key markets.

---

How do you know if you are winning or losing? While there are philosophical discussions about creating win-win scenarios in business, if the company is not profitable long term it is losing and will go out of business. Unless your company is a charitable organization, you had better be making a profit.

Notice first of all we are talking about long-term profitability. The company may take on a long-term investment with the knowledge their return will be two to ten years out. One of the big issues driving large companies is the need to show quarterly profits. Having a long-term investment which reduces profitability in the short term generally won't be accepted by the shareholders. Shareholders want their money to make money. Now. It is one of the few places a small to medium business has the advantage. The closely held corporation can take a long-term view and not be removed from managing the operation by the shareholders like in a large company.

## Market indicators

Is your business closely tied to a commodity or business sector? If your company has more than 35% of its production going to one sector, your company may be at risk. The automotive industry is cyclical. Typically, automobiles  will do well for about five years and then sales will take a nosedive. Oil and gas were bubbles no one thought would break, at least until they crashed in 2015. Construction is another big market driver that crashed in 2008.

Externally, a company should track key markets that influence their sales. Internally, the company should track the percentage of production tied to various market shares. Another chestnut: don't put all your eggs in one basket.

## Real life example

While working for an automotive supplier, I audited a fastener manufacturer on the West Coast. The owner of the fastener firm was an interesting individual. He started out manufacturing for aerospace but wisely identified his vulnerability. He diversified by selling into the automotive markets as well as other sectors. When the airline industry stopped buying planes, his competitors went out of business. While his company's profitability slipped, he remained in business. When aerospace roared back and the plane manufacturers were clamoring for approved fasteners, this business owner was there to fill the demand at a significant profit. The comment he made to me was he would never allow his company to be totally dependent on a single business.

## The Cost of Quality

There are two parts to the cost of quality. They are the cost of doing it right and the cost of doing it wrong. Thank Philip Crosby for promoting this concept. As a business owner you cannot afford to drive one down at the expense of increasing the other. It does not pay to add inspection to sort out non-conforming parts.

When I visit with clients, most track their non-conformances pretty well. They track external non-conformances the best with a structured complaint and response system. Little slips through without a response. That response does not always include prevention, but the company has a concept of how happy or unhappy their customers are.

Internal non-conformances are not always as closely watched as external non-conformances. They frequently go on the Thanksgiving turkey principle; drop a slice of turkey on the floor and you throw it away. Drop the whole turkey on the floor, pick it up, brush it off, and put it back on the platter. If a few pieces of the order are lost, drop them in the scrap bin without recording it, but  if the whole order is rejected, record it and look for a solution.

The cost few companies consider is the cost of prevention. They look at me like my dog when I say "cookie" but don't come up with the treat—confused. Prevention is just a cost of doing business, so why track it? Why, indeed.

Back in the 1970s it was normal to sort product and add inspectors when there was a problem. Think about the medical device company and the crew of inspectors checking plating. That was the normal way of doing business. If a company was delivering 95% good product they were doing a stellar job and the customer paid for it.

> The late 1970s and early 1980s was a revolution in the way businesses looked at quality. The Japanese were able to eliminate costs and increase profitability using quality. Deming and Juran were brought back to the USA and businesses started to listen to them. Philip Crosby was part of this revolution and tried to make systems which were statistically based more understandable with his book "Quality Is Free". It is still worth reading today.

In the 1980s along came the Japanese under the guidance of Deming, Juran, Crosby, and Taguchi, and the concept of high quality and low cost. Suddenly the new normal was 99.9996%

good product. Inspection added cost and was only 85% effective. Companies rushed to invest capital in automated inspection machines and training in specialty programs such as Lean or Six Sigma. Most companies didn't add the costs of these programs to the cost of quality. Once more, they are considered a cost of doing business, so why track them?

Each and every cost takes away from the bottom line. If the company uses less materials, labor, electricity, water, and basic overhead but produces the same quantity and quality of product, the company will increase profits. Quality systems utilize resources, just like production, finance, and management. Each and every one of those costs must be regularly reviewed to prevent bloat and waste even though they are a cost of doing business. Always question everything.

> **Real life example**
> In his first term as president, George Washington took no salary, merely asking that his expenses be covered by the fledgling country. His lavish dinner parties and entertainments were a cost of doing business and significantly higher than his proposed salary. When elected for the second time, Congress insisted George take a salary and pay his own expenses. It was a significantly lower cost for the taxpayers.

## Organizing the Cost of Quality Report

Below you will find a sample of a Cost of Quality report. Typically the report is organized with two sections, the cost of poor quality and the cost of prevention. These sections are added together for the total cost of quality. Wherever possible, take this information from existing reports. It reduces costs since efforts are not being duplicated and prevents meetings from digressing into whose figures are more accurate.

List the categories down the left side of the spreadsheet and the time frame across the top row. The first column is always the current month's data. Depending on the business the column next to it is either the previous

*Usually monthly reports are adequate to judge the health of a business but this too can be relative to the sales cycle. For the sake of clarity, I will use "monthly" here. Feel free to substitute what works best for your company.*

month's data or previous year's data. In cyclical businesses month-to-month comparisons do not mean as much as year-to-year. The last column is usually a year-to-date summary of the rows as compared to the previous year in the same time frame and

their percentage of the total cost of quality. Add the columns down to get the total monthly cost of quality. Add the row across to get a single category contribution.

Do not keep this report static. Add information and rows as data becomes available. Annotate the report so increases due to new categories are not misinterpreted. Annotate where actions were taken that reduced the Cost of Quality.

*After WWII manufacturers faced a high demand for consumer goods. If they could get it off the end of the production line, someone was waiting to buy it. The motto was caveat emptor, "buyer beware". Good quality was expensive and buyers paid more for it. Quality was looked at as a cost that reduced profitability unless it could be passed on to the consumer. Quality occurred with the addition of inspectors sorting good from bad.*

## Cost of Poor Quality

| Month | Current month | Previous month | Year-to-date | | Previous YTD | |
|---|---|---|---|---|---|---|
| | | | $ | % of TCOQ | $ | % of TOCQ |
| Returns | | | | | | |
| Rejects | | | | | | |
| Customer visits/ service calls | | | | | | |
| Rework | | | | | | |
| Inventory | | | | | | |
| Downtime | | | | | | |
| Warranty | | | | | | |
| Total | | | | | | |

## Cost of Good Quality

| Design review | | | | | | |
|---|---|---|---|---|---|---|
| Inspection | | | | | | |
| Auditing | | | | | | |
| Training | | | | | | |
| Testing | | | | | | |
| Prevention | | | | | | |
| Improvement | | | | | | |
| Total | | | | | | |
| Total Cost of Quality (TOCQ) | | | | | | |

## Summary

- Track the trend in markets which influence your sales.
- Track the percentage of your production linked to a single market such as automotive, aerospace, construction, or oil and gas.
- Look to diversify your customer base if a single industry provides more than 35% of your sales.

- Track the Cost of Quality, both Poor Quality and Good Quality.
- The Cost of Quality report should not be static. Make changes, add data as your company grows and changes. Annotate the report.

# Chapter 4

What Do You Want to Be?

---
**Chapter in a Nutshell:**
Regularly review each
product line for cost
to manufacture and
profitability.

---

Do you remember being asked, "What do you want to be when you grow up?" That is a question you need to pose to your business. You have a core product line where you are one of the expert producers, and then there is the other stuff you make. You have to ask why you make that other stuff. Did you pick it up to pay the bills? Do you need it because your customers want a full line of products? Do you believe that is the direction your business will migrate?

Most businesses start with an individual with a good idea supplying a need. The business may begin its life in a garage with the entrepreneur working nights while keeping their day job. Eventually this becomes a full time operation. The new business owner will put up their home as collateral to a bank to get working capital and hire on a few employees.

> One of the things to look at before pledging your personal assets is to see if you qualify for a Small Business Administration loan (SBA). The interest rate will be higher but your home will not be at risk. Also talk to your attorney about issues with mixing personal and corporate assets and what are the liabilities and consequences you might face.

When business falls off or a client is late in paying, the business owner takes on business that may not be their specialty, but keeps the doors open. It may be similar but different, such as a hiking boot manufacturer taking on a line of high heels. The secondary product line may have very low profit margins, but it covers payroll and keeps the bank from taking the owner's house. This may lead to a line of cowboy boots, then running shoes, until our hiking boot manufacturer manufactures shoes although their real strength and knowledge base is in manufacturing hiking boots.

Over time business grows. Employees are added. Accounts receivable replaces the owner's home as collateral. Still, sales are seldom looked at for their ability to generate profit. Cash flow is king and as long as money rolls in and product rolls out the compa-

> A banker in our networking group advised companies to get approved for lines of credit equal to 10-20% of sales before it was needed. There might be a small annual fee. However, it is usually easier to get credit when you don't need it than when you do need it.

ny waits until the end of the year to determine if they made a profit and how much.

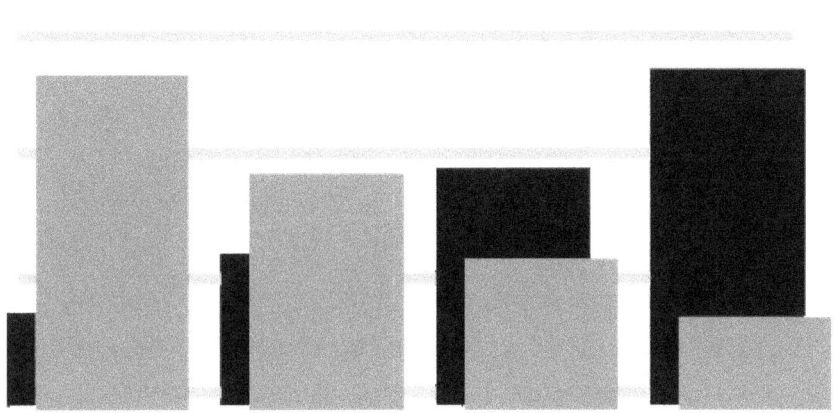

The dark bars in this graph are the gross sales while the light are the bottom-line profit for the company. Sales dollars are going up while profits are going down.

There is a theory that if a business isn't growing it is a matter of time until they go out of business. This leads to companies stretching outside their comfort zone for increased sales, not profits, and that is just as dangerous to the existence of the business as stagnation.

## Product Mix

What happens when there is a shift in business? This can happen gradually or suddenly. Sales of products with a good profit drop off, and products that just cover the bills increase. Now the business is using up equipment but not generating the profits needed to pay for a replacement. How early or late the business owner realizes this can have a significant impact on whether the company stays open or goes out of business.

## Real life example

A very large manufacturer of exhaust fans hired me. On some product lines the company was selling with a huge profit, others were selling with a loss. When seasonal shifts in the product mix occurred, the company went from significant profits to borderline running in the red. But they had no idea which were the big profit makers and which were selling for a loss. They had to wait until the end of a month to find out if they made money or not. The issue, in their case, turned out to be very inaccurate labor standards. Since overhead was calculated as a function of labor, the errors were a double whammy. With accurate labor standards they could develop the right price and consequently the fluctuations in profitability were decreased.

## What Are We Paying?

The first place is to look for accurate costs. Most companies know the purchase component cost of a product from their bills of material. The place where they have problems is in the labor. Developing accurate labor standards is critical to accurate costing. If employees are paid on piece rate, paychecks can fluctuate drastically depending on what is being manufactured. This is not good for long-term morale. If they are paid by the hour the output per day can shift drastically. You need to choose the one that makes the most sense for both you and your employees.

Overhead is assigned relative to labor. Therefore, overall costs can swing like a pendulum and management will have no idea if their projects are working or not.

## What Is Our Price?

While working in the pharmaceutical industry before
generics were popular, the
price of a product was simple. Double the cost and that
was the list price. Much of
that has changed, but it is not
unusual to utilize costs to determine price.

### Real life example

While I was still a fairly wet-behind-the-ears engineer, I went to work for a medical device company
as a process engineer. The company was fairly large
with 1,000 employees, but still family owned and run.
My job was to address any hiccups in production,
minimize the non-conforming material, and get things
running so product went out the door on time. The
company didn't believe in labor standards. In management's opinion the employees were hard-work-
ing, honest people so labor standards were unnecessary. More as a courtesy than anything else, I was
invited to a meeting to roll out a new laryngoscope.
It was priced at $25 per unit. I raised my hand and
said it cost more than that to make the product. I was
met with skepticism and directed to prove my point. I
followed the product through the manufacturing process and found it cost the company $125 to make the
product. They came very close to handing out $100
bills to each customer simply because they didn't
want to know what the labor cost per product was.

Another method of pricing is to use "what the market will bear." This usually results in wide variation of profitability. It also makes a product line vulnerable to competitors with an improvement that reduces costs and allows them to undersell everyone else.

### Real life example

There were two coffee shops in the Chicagoland area. Both were national chains but one was significantly larger than the other. In general people preferred the smaller chain's product and for a time that chain saw significant growth. The larger chain decided to make an aggressive move to stop the interloper. They went to the landlords of the smaller chain shops and offered a significantly increased amount of rent for the space. As leases came up, the smaller chain didn't have the cash reserves to pay the higher rents and still keep their prices the same. A few of their facilities tried raising the prices, resulting in a fall off of business. The smaller chain was forced to retreat from the Chicago area. The larger chain kept prices the same but reduced the size of their drinks and when the leases were up negotiated lower rents. The consumer lost, the small chain lost, and big business scored one.

## The Economics of Margins When There is Capacity

Suppose a company has looked at their product lines and understands the variations in product profitability. While there are products with low to break-even profits, they are able to make them with their in-house expertise and with no additional investment over the high profit products. Should they drop the low-profit product?

Not if they have available capacity. If they have machinery idle on their normal working shifts and can manufacture the low profit products then they should continue to make them.

If they have to add shifts or are at maximum capacity then it is time to consider dropping the product line. The reason is the distribution of overhead. By spreading the overhead across more products the contribution to each is smaller. Smaller overhead allows for more profit.

### Real life example

A client asked me to develop labor standards. They were a highly automated operation. When I went in on third shift, I found a single operator. All set ups were done on first and second shift. The machines were left to run through the third shift with the primary focus of the third shift operator on daily maintenance issues. The lights, heat, water, etc. had to be on for the operator on third shift so any parts made required no additional fixed cost and no additional labor. This made it feasible to run low margin products during the third shift.

## Full Service

Sometimes a company has to provide lower margin prod-ucts in order to keep clients who purchase high profit products happy. A company may manufacture a range of parts very efficiently; how-ever, products outside that  range require special equipment and skill sets. Their customers want to go to one place and order all of that product line. In order to keep customers of their key business, the company will either outsource or manufacture the remaining products at a loss.

### Real life example

A client wanted me to build labor standards for their woodworking clamps. The products were made of wood and steel and very high quality and durable. They sold to specialty shops and big box home im-provement stores. To keep the home improvement stores happy, they needed to provide a low-cost range of clamps as well. The low-cost clamps were molded plastic, an expense and technology they were not familiar with utilizing. They decided to go offshore to buy these products to supply them to the big box store. From a business standpoint this was a good decision, but they did get caught in the trap discussed in "Anchors Away."

## So what?

Perhaps you already knew everything in this section. How does any of this help? The answer is simple. Knowledge is power. You have to decide if it makes more sense to drop lines and use the resources to build your core business, outsource elements outside your core business, or find a way to make the periphery products profitable. The knowledge will help you decide where to spend your resources. Recognize this isn't a one and done effort. As projects are implemented and, as industry shifts, this is a study which must be repeated at regular intervals and decisions made based on it for the long-term health of the business.

Companies must track product mix, analyze shifts, and determine their course of action. This may or may not mean dropping whole product lines. The business must decide what they are good at manufacturing and what they aren't, and decide if they need to get into or out of the things that are not their core products.

Ultimately, the owner or manager must look at regular reports by product line on profitability versus capacity and their trends. The sample report below is based on quarterly data for profitability. Depending on the company's sales cycle this may need to be revised to monthly or annually. The final column is the most important one to focus on. Is the change in profitability increasing or decreasing? The why is as important as the amount of change.

Again, don't let your staff pick the fly poop out of the pepper to generate the report, but the data should be accurate. If as a company it is not possible to attribute the costs to a specific product, this is a point to step back and think about what data is collected, and how to get this information. Just because the Bill of Material attributes a level of labor doesn't make it reality. A manager should not have to wait until the end of the month to find out if the company made or lost money.

Again, keep it simple. It is usually easier to keep capacity and profitability separate. In profitability it is important to look not only at the current position but also the trends.

| Product | Current quarter | | | | | | Previous Quarter | | | |
|---|---|---|---|---|---|---|---|---|---|---|
| | Materials | Labor | Attributed Overhead | Total | Price | Potential Profit | Total | Price | Potential Profit | Change in Profit |
| Widget A | | | | | | | | | | |
| Widget B | | | | | | | | | | |
| Widget C | | | | | | | | | | |
| Widgets Total | | | | | | | | | | |
| Gizmo A | | | | | | | | | | |
| Gizmo B | | | | | | | | | | |
| Gizmo C | | | | | | | | | | |
| Gizmo Total | | | | | | | | | | |

## Summary

- Companies must determine and regularly review the cost to manufacture and the profitability of their products.
- Companies must understand the relationship of their products to their core skills and their customer base.
- Low profit products, the ones that pay for overhead without increasing costs, should continue to be manufactured until the plant is at full capacity.
- If a product does not produce an acceptable profit, the company must determine if they need to provide the product or drop it. There are good reasons to do both.
- The company must look at the entire impact of outsourcing versus manufacturing marginal products. This goes beyond pricing and profit issues.

# Chapter 5

Mikey

A long time ago there was an advertisement for a cereal. Two children, suspicious of the taste of a healthy breakfast, gave it to Mikey since he would eat anything. There is a similarity between Mikey and some employees. It is key employee syndrome.

**How Do You Know?**

Does your company have key employee syndrome? Here is a simple test. Create a spreadsheet of all the projects currently planned or under way and the team members. Now sort on the team member names. Does one person appear on all or most of those teams? Is it you? Now look at who is integral to each company department. Does one name keep popping up? Look at your organizational chart. Is someone holding multiple positions? If in any of these cases there was that one person, then your company has key employee syndrome.

> ### Real life example
> I audited a client to ISO 9001 prior to quoting a revamping of the QMS. When I got to production there was a singular dearth of documentation. The source of all information was the manufacturing manager. Trying to bring home the weakness, I asked what the company did when the manufacturing manager went on vacation. Shutdown? The answer, "Yes, why is that a problem?"

## Is It a Problem?

Probably. If the key employee is sitting on every team and every committee to stay informed, then the impact is minimal. How they are getting their own work done is another question.

Some people will spend their day in meetings and their nights playing catch up on their own work. It isn't good for their health or their family and is only a short term positive for the company. This is the recipe for that employee to fall over with a heart attack. Those situations are seldom good for morale or productivity. It may feel like the company has a great employee, but long-term costs are significant.

Your business is in danger if this person makes all the decisions. You are not getting the full benefit of the other people you hired.

The key employee makes all the decisions and the others soon learn, "Why bother offering new ideas?"

The next generation has limited opportunity to stretch and learn. That young engineer fresh out of college turns into a clerk or a CAD operator doing the tasks they are told to perform but not understanding why or being allowed to present new things they learned in college.

It won't take long for the people with potential to leave and only those biding time to remain. When the key employee leaves, retires, or drops dead no one is trained to pick up the pieces and keep the business going.

### Real life example

There was a manufacturer of fine china. They had an outstanding engineer on the payroll. The man was able to automate processes that had been done manually for hundreds of years. He was a magician at keeping those machines running. Pricing and staffing were based on those machines working. The engineer died in an auto accident. That is when the owner found out there were no drawings for the machines and no one trained to fix them. They came very close to going out of business.

## Control Freak

When looking at your key employee analysis, was it your name that kept popping up? As a business owner you have the biggest stake in seeing that the business remains successful. When the business was started with that super nifty new process, no one could do

it as well as you. As employees are added, you can't seem to find anyone who does the job as well as you did it, but you can't do it all. So you spend long hours checking and correcting how things are done.

Stop. Ask yourself why you are working. To provide for your family? If you have a heart attack or stroke and you are the only one who knows how to manage the business, what will happen to them then? Do you want to leave something behind as a legacy? Unless you let people help, you are limiting the growth of your company and your legacy won't last long. The very best thing you can do is train the next leader and force yourself to find an outside interest.

## What Do You Do About It?

Whether the key employee is the business owner or a manager working for the owner, action is necessary. Start with evaluating the strengths and weaknesses of the key employee and what parts of the business make the key employee excited. Is this someone who loves new technology? Do they love getting their hands covered with machining lubricant and measuring up a part? That is the area to channel the key employee into, and all other areas should go away.

Do not call the key employee in and tell them you are taking away responsibilities and titles. Bring them in and ask them to give you a plan of what they would do if they could focus entirely on their favorite area.

Utilize the desire to implement that plan. Ask the key employee to identify candidates for the other tasks not related to the favorite area. There will be resistance. Get the key employee to develop a job description for all their other responsibilities or positions. Try to identify candidates to fit these job descriptions.

Requiring the key employee to be a mentor may or may not work. Not everyone can teach. Allow other employees to step up and modify the position into something they can make successful. Short term this will  be very frustrating, but for a small- to medium-sized business, the long-term effect is what matters.

If the business owner is that key employee, it is time for some planning. Where do you want the business to be in five years? What part of being an owner do you hate? What information do you need in order to be comfortable with the things you are delegating to lead to your five-year goals? What is your exit strategy? Because with you as the key employee, your retirement or demise will pretty much mean closing the doors and chaining them shut when you leave.

Which employees could step up? If no one can step up, what training do they need to get there? Lay out where you want to be, what needs to happen to get there, and define goals and

objectives for the people to whom you are going to delegate responsibilities to accomplish. See if they have input that will help
accomplish those goals faster. Then take up a hobby that will
force you out of the office. Whether it is cooking lessons with
your spouse, ballroom dancing classes, combat pistol shooting,
hunting, fishing—you name it. Be unavailable for a few hours
every week and force people to step up while making a way for
you to step down.

## Summary

- Identify your key employees.
- Recognize that key employees hinder, not help, the growth of your business.
- Look at the key employee's strength and business passion to create positive growth for the company.
- Identify your five-year vision and plan how you are going to use your employees to get there.
- If you are the key employee, ask yourself why and figure out a plan to fix it.

# Chapter 6

Flavor of the Month

---

**Chapter in a Nutshell:**
Select the right system for the company and give it time to work.

---

Major initiatives can be good or bad for the company and bottom line profits. If focused and well-implemented they are dynamic tools to long-term improvement. If poorly supported and resourced, they drain day-to-day operations, reduce profits, and show little to no results. Keeping long-term major projects fresh year after year is also difficult. They become part of the mundane daily activities that must be accomplished but will soon lack enthusiasm and energy.

### Real life example

I worked at a company that made me hate *Inc. Magazine*. My boss had a subscription, and he took every article as the source for all future profit improvement ideas. Each month there would be an article about a business system, and within a week the management staff would be directed to implement it. Before we could get started, the next magazine would come out and we would have a new project added to our plates without the previous activities being taken away. When we did not get the results demonstrated in the article in a matter of weeks, it was reflected in our raises and bonuses. It didn't take long for people with good skills and resumes to leave.

The problem with the "flavor of the month" style of management is that it saps resources and creates skepticism and resistance to change. It rewards passive aggressive behavior. If the employees don't like the new concept, they can ignore it and wait to get behind the next big idea without a lot of concern.

## Patience

Remember the things needed for a project to be successful are time, scope, and resources. Implementing Lean or Six Sigma or an ISO standard will take some of the company's limited resources. In order for the project to be successful, enough time and resources need to be allocated along with the clearly defined expectations to be accomplished. The time to accomplish the implementation such that results are achieved takes months, or possibly years, even if the sales cycle is very short. To achieve long-term results the project has to be viewed and planned over a number of years. Of course this is where the small to medium business has an advantage. The shareholders are generally closely affiliated with the business and more open to a longer wait for a return on their investment.

## Changing the Culture

Most significant system changes require a change in culture and that is not easy to accomplish. People are comfortable with their existing methods. Change feels awkward and uncomfortable, sometimes even frightening.

What is culture? It is the shared experiences, education and habits of a group of individuals working and/or living together. It is a way of thinking, behaving or working that exists in a place or organization.

Exercise pundits tell us that we must incorporate a changed behavior in our routine for 21 days in order for it to become habit. The same is true when asking people to change how they do their jobs.

Peer pressure can be significant. If a peer leader whom the employees trust is not in favor of the change, the people in their sphere of influence will be unsupportive as well. If it is supported there will still be confusion. When do employees bring something up? Will it impact their career if they point out a problem or concern? If the new system fails, how will it affect them? There is a strong component of fear that must be addressed by telling the employees what they will gain personally if the system is successful.

## Trusted Peers

Many times an owner or manager has a peer group they trust and talk to about the problems they face. It is a group of like-minded individuals facing similar challenges. However, it can also cause problems. Someone in  that group may have had a wonderful experience with a business system or read a book that had all the secrets to running a business. Since this is a trusted peer group the owner may think, "It worked for them, it will work for me." They buy copies of the book and distribute them to their staff telling them, "We are going to do this."

This creates several problems. First, the two businesses are seldom the same. Issues, customer base, and sales cycle are all different, causing the system's effectiveness to be significantly different.

The second problem is a lack of knowledge of the new system. Reading a book, taking a seminar, or watching a video is not going to give your staff the information or experience to deal with all the things that will come up.

The third problem is finding an in-house champion for the project. This isn't just a matter of understanding. The champion must truly believe the system will make a difference and have the respect of their peers to be able to influence them.

## Hiring a Consultant

There are consultants who borrow your watch to tell you the time. They bring nothing to the project other than a big invoice.

Other consultants can be the difference in your system change being a success or a failure. How do you know if the consultant is worth hiring or not?

First look for experience and time in the field. It would be nice if they are familiar with the nuances of your industry, but what is more important is that they have the skills and experience in the system they are implementing. Find  out how long they have been making a living doing this type of implementation. If they have been able to support themselves for several years, chances are they have been pretty successful at other places.

Are they staying current with changes? When was the last time they either took or taught a course on the system? Maybe they are published in trade magazines. All of this will tell you if you have someone who will bring energy and focus to your implementation or simply coast and collect checks.

Ask for references. Is there a client willing to vouch for their effectiveness? You can check out their profile on a business social media site such as LinkedIn for references and history. Of course no consultant is going to give you the names of unhappy clients or post bad reviews, so ask around your peer group and see if anyone has experiences they will share.

## Maintaining Energy Year After Year

When a company correctly implements systems such as ISO 9001, ISO 14001, or World Class Manufacturing, a lot of energy and excitement develop. Everyone has expectations as to how the system will benefit both the company and them as individuals. Once the systems are incorporated into day-to-day activities and the process has been in place for a few years, the initial excitement can wane.

Here is where the Cost of Quality report can help. It should be published and posted for all to see. Goals to improve it need to be set, but the goals must be both achievable and innovative. Rewards and/or recognition are necessary every time an incremental improvement is made. Recognize that, as time goes on and low hanging fruit is collected, it will become more difficult and consume more resources to create the same incremental levels of improvement.

Here is where the leadership skills of management are tested. First they must identify reasonable projects to be accomplished.

Second they must evaluate proposed projects and clearly communicate when the return on the investment isn't there to make it worth expending the resources. They must explain, in terms the workforce understands, why the project will not benefit them as employees.

Third, they must be cheerleaders for new projects even when the return is smaller than for earlier projects. The support can't be faked. The attitude of management must be positive without being false. The leadership must communicate, "This isn't as big a change as some of our other past projects, but it will be valuable and we want it to be implemented."

### Real life example

The management of one of my clients saw the value of conservation early on. If they could use less material, energy, water, etc. to make the same number of parts they would increase profitability. They did a number of projects with significant changes to the bottom line. After a few years, a client demanded they become ISO 14001 certified. When it came to continuing improvements there was a declining margin of value which both the client and the auditor questioned. Thankfully they had documentation of the changes they had made ahead of their competition and there was no issue with the client or the auditor.

## Summary

- Systems implementations must be managed, including allowing the time for them to be productive.
- Changing systems at short intervals does more harm than good.
- New systems must always be looked at for what they will do for the company before being implemented.
- The right consultant will help make the project successful.
- Not all consultants are created equal.
- The difficulty is not in implementation of a new system but in maintaining it.

# Chapter 7

Alligator Alley

**Chapter in a Nutshell:**
Various tools to analyze and prevent issues.

When you are up to your ears in alligators it is difficult to remember your original objective was to drain the swamp. When unhappy clients are calling faster than you can deal with a situation, implementing a quality system seems to be the last thing a company can do.

Remember the word *triage*? It occurs when there are more injuries than people to treat them. This is where you take

> Prevention is making it harder to do it wrong than it is to do it right.

a lesson from the medical profession and sort for the most serious problems first. If you have a non-functioning part with liability risks, it has to get the resources over a billing error with a credit less than postage to mail a check.

What needs to happen is more than a band-aid fix. Yes, the unhappy customer needs to be made whole, or as whole as the company can. However, the company cannot stop there. The management must focus on prevention.

Prevention is not "re-train the operator." When an auditor reads that on corrective actions, their natural reaction is to start digging and come up with a whole pile of findings.

The first place the auditor will go is to find out how the system allowed poorly trained operators to work with inadequate supervision. They will look for training frequency. They will then dig into the production records for every place that operator made the part and ask how the company knows that production was to specification. They will look at acceptance criteria for shipment. They will look for recall procedures and traceability. In general, "re-train the operator" is an invitation to be invasively evaluated with a microscope.

Prevention is sometimes called foolproofing. It is making it so an operator must almost deliberately act improperly to make the product incorrectly.

When high-risk non-conformance gets into the field, the primary focus must be on not letting it happen again. It follows the old saying, "fool me once, shame on you, fool me twice, shame on me."

Prevention doesn't stop at the single failure of the QMS. What are the related products, or products manufactured with the same process? Are they at risk of the same failure? In order to stop shooting the alligators, action must be taken to lower the water level so the alligators have no place to live. **The system has to be changed so it is easier to make the part *to* specifications than *not* to specifications.**

### Blaming the Operator
Dr. Juran had a simple test for determining if an error was operator-controlled. He asked:

- Does the operator have the ability to know [easily] if the product is good or bad?
- If the product is bad, does the operator have the knowledge and ability to adjust the process to make good parts?

If either of those tests fails, don't blame the operator.

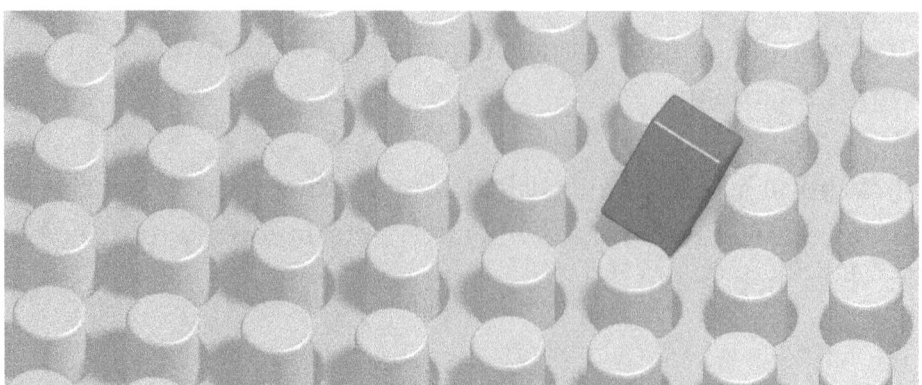

The ability of the operator to know if they are making conforming or non-conforming parts has two elements: knowledge and access. If a simple visual inspection or handheld device (e.g., a test fixture, micrometer, or caliper) can be used to measure conformance, and the employee knows how to use it, then the employee has the ability to determine conformance versus non-conformance on their own.

If a laboratory test is necessary, or the employee has to leave the workstation for such a long time that it impacts productivity to determine conformance, then the employee doesn't have the ability to determine if a product is bad or good. If the employee hasn't been trained on how the test is performed and what it means in terms of conformance, then the employee doesn't have the ability to determine conformance.

### Real life example

A plastic injection molding company had a plant in Mexico that ran on three shifts. The plant was based near one of their highest-volume customer's facilities. The customer was very upset at receiving non-conforming parts intermittently in boxes. I went in and looked at the operation. Observing the day shift, the parts were to print and the controlling parameters followed. Second shift performed the same. No one understood the cause of the problem until I went in on third shift. Once the operators got over the shock of a boss lady showing up at night, they proudly showed me how they had to adjust the machines due to the cooler night temperatures. What they didn't know was their adjustments impacted other part dimensions. Before leaving, they readjusted the controls back to those they had been directed to use so things would be ready for the first shift. They were trying to make the best parts possible but didn't have the knowledge to understand they were making non-conforming parts. We got in a team of engineers to work with quality and the operators to develop sliding scales of adjustments depending on atmospheric conditions, and gave them an inspector to check all dimensions after an adjustment.

If an employee can be fairly confident that the non-conforming issue either won't be detected in the next operation, or can't be traced back to them, or believes it is not an important characteristic, then there is the possibility they will knowingly continue to produce non-conforming parts.

### Real life example

At a plastic injection molding company a customer demanded less than 4 PPM non-conforming parts. The customer's reasoning was sound. They were running 32 million of the parts per week on a line with 7 people. When one of the parts was non-conforming it caused them a 10-minute shutdown for everyone to clean up spills, so every non-conforming part cost them over an hour of labor. The manufacturing manager thought the demand was ridiculous. This, of course, resulted in a faceoff between the manufacturing manager and the quality manager. Significant testing to detect the non-conformance was implemented while waiting for long-term solutions to be put in place. This resulted in a high level of rejected material. Instead of re-grinding the product, the production manager had third shift re-label the boxes and slip them into the pallets after inspection. What he didn't count on was the quality manager regularly appearing on third shift. The supervisor was not comfortable with their subterfuge and communicated to the quality manager what was happening. Corrective action was implemented. A secondary operation was added and the problem product became a shining example of Six Sigma project success for the production manager.

If the employee has met the first criteria (can determine conformance or non-conformance) and has the training to adjust the process to make good parts then they meet the second criteria for operator error. This includes stopping the machine and calling for action without repercussions.

This is a place where piecework can create a problem. If the operator is paid by productivity they feel the pinch in their wallet for stopping production. Being able to clock off the job is only going to be supported by the operator if there is another position to clock onto. Otherwise they are going to tweak and create temporary fixes which may have other negative results.

### Real life example

An employee was charged with cleaning resistors with a tumbler. A certain percentage of parts had to be reprocessed because there was a residue on the finished parts. The operator theorized that increasing the amount of soap being used in the tumbler would do a better job of cleaning. The residue was actually from the soap and parts not being thoroughly rinsed. The change made by the operator made the problem worse.

## Design Review

How does a business owner or manager get past the alligators?

Prevention starts in design with the design review. Most business owners and many managers look at this as a waste of time but that is one of the biggest mistakes they can make. The original moves in a design determine future costs and manufacturability. When the idea starts, it is a concept on paper. The company has invested in time from the designer but no other resources. Errors here are easy to fix. The later in the design cycle the problem is found, the more costly it is to correct.

### Real life example

A pharmaceutical manufacturer tasked an engineer to design a filling line for their new cough syrup. The engineer carefully designed each workspace on the line and arranged for appropriate queuing space. Before being allowed to order the equipment, we held a design review. Unfortunately the engineer had failed to take into account the size of the facility. If his design was built, the company would have been packing the bottles of syrup across the street in the tractor supply showroom.

The first step in the design review is to demonstrate whether the design meets the requirements of the project while still on paper (or computer screen). The change costs at this point are minimal. In the example above, the line was turned several times to keep it inside the building. Additional input was able to reduce the line length and number of work stations as well.

### Real life example

A client called me in and tasked me with designing a machine to assemble a cord to a heating element. Part of the problem was the space I had to work with and the staffing I would be allowed to use. I had 10 feet x 5 feet and two operators to accomplish the assembly of the cord and the packing and palletizing of the parts. No design reviews were performed so no one checked the power requirements. If they had done the design review, they would have noticed the power cord was missing. Instead of having a well-designed line, there was significant added cost to bring me in after the project was supposed to be complete to design an automated machine for the cramped space.

One of the great things about using computer aided design (CAD) is the immediate indication of interference issues and tolerance build up. Prior to CAD this was done manually and was a long and laborious process. The design should still be reviewed for tolerance build ups, unit of measure issues, and interference fits, but the tools of design have made this much easier to deal with and to prevent issues.

Once the design is on paper it is time to bring in interested parties for manufacturability. It is important to get supplier input at this point in the process. This input is valuable in minimizing material costs.

### Real life example

A public building was on the drafting board. The architect had a gorgeous design for the food court. Everything was one-of-a-kind manufacture to print elements and the overall cost to build it was going to be between $3-5 million. The budget was for $1.5 million. There was serious discussion of scrapping the entire design. However, when the contractor was given leeway to order similar off-the-shelf parts, the actual building costs were brought down to $1 million and the architect got the design he envisioned.

Manufacturing should be included in the design review. They know what processes create the non-conformances and quality will have records of field failures. Designing for manufacturability reduces costs and increases profitability over the long term.

### Real life example

A company was a first tier automotive supplier and bringing on a new item to a product line. The material at a fastener was reduced to half due to the bolt hole. Accompanying this was poor repeatability by the punching equipment since the surface was curved and tended to move in the fixture. The combined issues resulted in field failures due to fatigue at the fastener. While a project was proposed to improve repeatability at the punch fixturing, it was a low priority project. The curve of the surface was for aesthetics. By making the surface flat, the part could be better located in the punch with significant improvement to

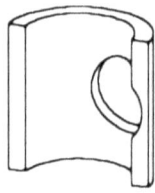 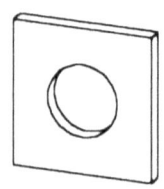

repeatability. Field failures for this item was a factor of 10 less than all other members of the product line. The other parts in the line were gradually converted to flat surfaces as the tooling needed replacing. Since the new product was fixed before the tool was manufactured significant costs were saved.

Design reviews should be at logical intervals. This is going to differ from industry to industry. What is logical is to do design reviews at the concept stage, the completed concept stage and before tooling, at the testing stage, and as a final review when everything is completed. A company can design their own form or search for them on the internet. There are several good ones out there.

## Failure Mode and Effect Analysis (FMEA)

FMEA, not to be confused with FEMA (Federal Emergency Management Agency) is where the business taps into its tribal knowledge. Look at the new product. For most companies there are similarities to other products they manufacture. There is both a design FMEA and a process FMEA.

The design FMEA looks at the parts themselves and the design. Where could this part go wrong? Ask, "if the hole must be centered +/- .005 inch, what if it isn't?" rather than "The part moves in the fixturing, what happens if the hole is off-center?"

FMEA was one of the first systematic techniques for failure analysis. It was developed by reliability engineers in the 1950's to study problems which might arise from malfunctions of military systems. A FMEA is often the first step of a system reliability study. It involves reviewing as many components, assemblies and sub-assemblies as possible to identify failure modes and their cause and effects.

**Potential**
**Failure Mode and Effects Analysis**
(Design FMEA)

System :
Subsystems :
Component :
Model Year / Vehicle (s) :
Core Team :

Design Responsibility :
Key Date :

FMEA Number :
Prepared by :
FMEA Date (Orig.) :          (Rev.) :

| Item / Function | Potential Failure Mode | Potential Effects of Failure | Severity | Class | Potential Causes / Mechanisms of Failure | Current Design Controls Prevention | Occurrence | Current Design Controls Detection | Detect | R.P.N. | Recommended Actions | Responsibility & Target Completion Date | Actions Taken | Severity | Occur | Detection | R.P.N. |
|---|---|---|---|---|---|---|---|---|---|---|---|---|---|---|---|---|---|
| | | | | | | | | | | | No action required | | | | | | |
| | | | | | | | | | | | No action required | | | | | | |
| | | | | | | | | | | | No action required | | | | | | |
| | | | | | | | | | | | No action required | | | | | | |
| | | | | | | | | | | | No action required | | | | | | |
| | | | | | | | | | | | No action required | | | | | | |
| | | | | | | | | | | | No action required | | | | | | |
| | | | | | | | | | | | No action required | | | | | | |
| | | | | | | | | | | | No action required | | | | | | |
| | | | | | | | | | | | No action required | | | | | | |
| | | | | | | | | | | | No action required | | | | | | |
| | | | | | | | | | | | No action required | | | | | | |
| | | | | | | | | | | | No action required | | | | | | |
| | | | | | | | | | | | No action required | | | | | | |
| | | | | | | | | | | | No action required | | | | | | |
| | | | | | | | | | | | No action required | | | | | | |
| | | | | | | | | | | | No action required | | | | | | |
| | | | | | | | | | | | No action required | | | | | | |
| | | | | | | | | | | | No action required | | | | | | |
| | | | | | | | | | | | No action required | | | | | | |
| | | | | | | | | | | | No action required | | | | | | |
| | | | | | | | | | | | No action required | | | | | | |
| | | | | | | | | | | | No action required | | | | | | |
| | | | | | | | | | | | No action required | | | | | | |

_(columns grouped under "Action Results" heading: Actions Taken, Severity, Occur, Detection, R.P.N.)_

The process FMEA looks at the manufacturing process and how to design prevention into the tooling and process. Here is where the team would ask, "If we make the hole off center what happens?"

To get started ask, "Where do we have problems we already know about?" It is the point in time where the team asks, "What if..." and lists potential failures. Start with the things that have gone wrong, or could go wrong. This will have a range of likelihood of happening from very rare–almost impossible to very easily–has happened in the past. These lists should not be limited. This is a brainstorming session. Limit the structuring and let ideas flow.

Once all the potential failure modes are listed, determine how the failure could affect the function. This could range from "no effect" to "cease to function" to "cause life-threatening injury."

Numerical values, usually from 1 to 10, are assigned relative to the severity of the failure; the more severe, the higher the number. There are a number of industry specific charts that guide the user on the severity number. If your industry does not have a specific one, then it is acceptable for you to determine your company's criteria. It is important that this range be reasonable. You know your industry best. The severity numbers should not be skewed to give either all high severity or all low severity. The FMEA is a tool and it is only useful if taken seriously.

From the potential failures possible causes are assigned. This is where the part slipping in the fixture comes into play. There could be multiple potential causes for a single failure. After listing the causes, their likelihood is assigned a number from 1 to 10. One is highly unlikely to occur, 10 is highly likely to occur.

The third step is to list the controls currently in place to prevent the failure due to the specific cause. If there is a 100% likelihood the failure will be detected and not get out of the facility, that is given a low number rating of 1. If there is no check to prevent the failure from getting to the customer, the assigned likelihood is 10.

At this point the FMEA starts to yield information. Calculate the severity times the occurrence [of the cause] times the [potential] detection. The higher this number the greater the risk of a customer getting a failed part.

The idea behind FMEA is not to attack every potential cause. The number where action needs to be taken varies depending on the industry. If it is determined action is needed, again, the group brainstorms what to do. An individual is assigned the responsibility to either analyze multiple potential solutions or to implement solutions. A time frame to complete the actions is set. The group reconvenes to follow up on the actions.

FMEAs consume a lot of resources. They should be done by a group, rather than an individual. If the decision is made not to implement some actions, the group should be made aware of the reason. Again, limited resources must be used wisely and this may be a valid reason for delaying actions. However, if future FMEAs are to provide value, the input must be taken seriously and reviewed at reasonable intervals.

## Process Flow Diagrams

Process Flow diagrams are the next step. How will the product be made, where are the checkpoints, and what are the decisions? It may be valuable to annotate where data is now collected for the decision points.

Look for places the process flows backwards. Look for choke points—steps in the process where only a small number of parts can get through. The rule of thumb is that capacity for the next

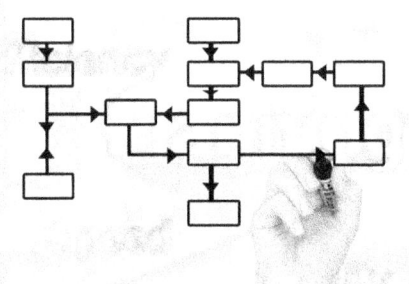

process step should be equal to or greater than the step before it.

### Real life example

We had a problem when making injectible medicines. At times we would have to either throw away parts of a batch or wait for packaging materials to be sterilized before batching.

The liquid medicine was batched in non-sterile conditions, then filtered for sterility. The containers to be filled needed to be autoclaved and every item going into the room had to be sterilized. After a specific number of hours there could be "grow-through" on the filters and any remaining medicine in the tank was no longer useable.

A single batch of packaging material going through the autoclave was not enough to process an order. Originally the production was balanced. However, new larger tanks were purchased and installed to increase throughput. A simple process flow diagram as part of the design review would have determined a larger autoclave was needed as well.

## Fishbone or Ishikawa Diagrams

This is the point in time where we switch from "big picture" generalizations to digging into the detail. We use fishbone or Ishikawa diagrams to address a specific problem or issue.

The head of the fish is the problem. Be specific as this can make a difference in the analysis and input of the group. For example, "50% of the widgets coming off the end of the line have scratches on the base" will help in the analysis. If we had said the widgets have scratches, the team would analyze all of the equipment instead of the parts of the process related to the base. By telling the team it is a localized problem the source tooling is examined.

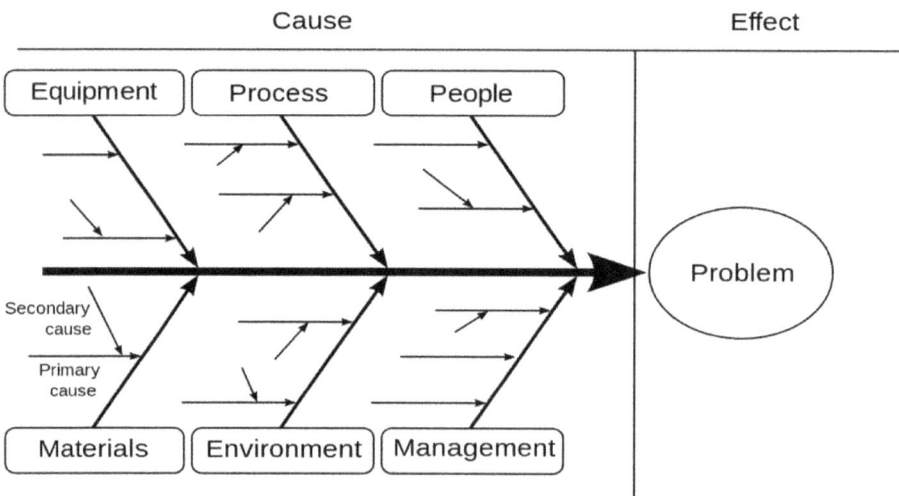

Once we have the head of the fish and draw the spine, we need to draw the ribs. It is perfectly reasonable to have any number of ribs. However, if people are unfamiliar with this brainstorming tool, and to confirm all sources are reviewed, most teams use 6 major ribs. To help in remembering them people frequently call them the 6 M's:

- Machines
- Methods (Process)
- Manpower (People)
- Materials
- Management
- Mother Nature (Environment)

It sometimes helps to list equipment, procedures, and suppliers next to the main rib. Now the rule is to ask why could the rib be the source of the non-conformance five times. There was a nice article on LinkedIn, which I shared to the Technacon Facebook page, which changed this to "What causes" or "What is the purpose." So if we look at equipment and ask, "What equipment could cause scratches in the base?" it focuses the resources in the meeting. Now the team should drill down four more levels. In the above example we could suggest "tool wear." Why is the tool wearing? "Not being lubricated properly," "slight changes in raw material properties," "not following maintenance procedures," etc.

Once the team has exhausted the brainstorming it is time to get to analysis. Usually there are more ideas than resources to fix the problem. Additionally, some ideas are more likely than others. Get agreement on how data is going to be gathered, for how long, and by whom. Set a date and time to reconvene and review the data.

The goal of the second meeting is to either identify reasonable actions or if the data indicates the source hasn't been identified, to perform additional analysis on some of the ideas that had not been addressed. If actions are identified, test them, check to see if they are an effective solution, and if so, fully implement them, i.e., follow Dr. Deming's Plan-Do-Check-Act.

**Real life example**

A client had a repetitive non-conformance from multiple customers for wrong count. We did a fishbone of where the contributors to this problem were. What we found was the following:

- Vibration from the machine shop caused erroneous readings of the scale. Counter scales were moved and dampeners added.
- Assembly scale counters were not sensitive enough for the parts being weighed. Scales were replaced.
- The shipping scale was getting icy blasts of cold air in the winter which caused inaccurate readings. The scale was moved.
- Operators would get interrupted during manual counts. Training was revised to always line up parts in rows of five.

Solutions reduced wrong counts by 80%.

## Turtle Diagrams

The Turtle diagram is used to understand a process rather than solve a problem. It is supposed to be a tool for auditors, but who says you can't use it? It takes into account the concept of supplier ⇨ input ⇨ process ⇨ output ⇨ customer series (SIPOC), which means every process has customers and suppliers, and combines it with the fishbone diagram.

If you are an automotive supplier, you are supposed to have one of these for every major process.

In the case of the turtle, the shell is the process and the activities involved are defined. The head of the turtle is the outputs. Some organizations keep the diagram simple—the assembly or subassembly name, documents, and waste, if any, such as runners or scrap steel. Others list who the customers are and their requirements. The purpose for using the turtle guides the most effective description

The tail is made up of the inputs, both materials and information, such as travelers, shop drawings, specifications, and who supplies them. The legs are similar to the ribs for the fishbone diagram: Procedures or Methods, Training or Manpower, Facilities or Machines, Performance Standards or Management. The materials rib is covered by the tail, and environment is included in facilities. Some people will title the sheet with the non-conformance and use the turtle as a problem-solving tool for non-conformances.

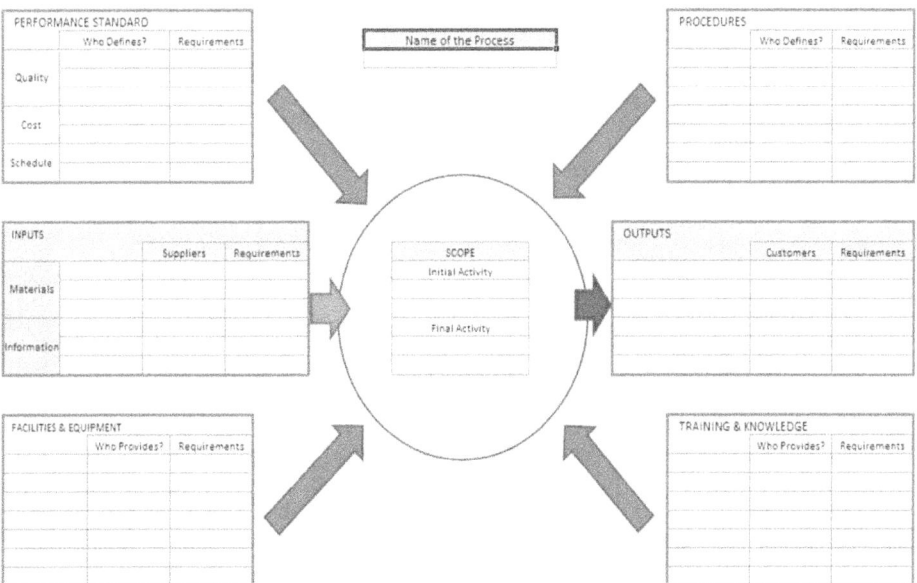

Rule of thumb: When analyzing a problem, use the fishbone. When analyzing a process, use the turtle. The turtle guides the user to look more closely at documentation on an intuitive basis, but both are effective if used correctly.

It is possible to link turtle diagrams so the output of one is the input of the other, to look at a process from beginning to the end. It can be a useful tool in identifying processes that have become non-value added or redundant. For example, filling out a form online and then printing it to give it to the next person.

### Real life example

A client had the order entry staff scan all faxes, and print and scan e-mails and attach them to the electronic file for any credits back to the customers. The entire file was then printed and passed from person to person for approvals. Once approved by at least four people the accounting department scanned everything in and saved it in the credit file along with a scan of the check. We had them save all the documents as PDFs without printing or scanning them afterwards, and then e-mail the credit file simultaneously to the approvers. They added electronic signatures and sent it on to accounting, who approved a bank transfer of funds. We saved days on the process and a small forest.

## Summary:

- Don't blame the operator unless they can actually do something about the problem.
- Start in the design stage looking for ways to prevent non-conformances and waste.

- Design review is an effective tool.
- FMEAs are worth doing right.
- Process flow diagrams identify wasted movement resulting in wasted labor and materials.
- Problem solving requires looking in more detail and at specific data.
- Fishbone diagrams work well for analyzing a single non-conformance.
- Turtle diagrams work well at analyzing a process.

# Chapter 8

Alphabet Soup

**Chapter in a Nutshell:**
The differences between Lean, Six Sigma, ISO 9001, and ISO 14001

Say the phrase "ISO 9001" and business owners give you a range of reactions from eye rolling that would do a teenager proud all the way to grins. The most common response is a stoic silence. The vast majority of clients look at the standard as a cost of doing business, not as a business tool.

There are a number of standards from Military Standards (MIL STD) to the International Organization for Standardization

(ISO) to specialty standards such as Technical Specification (TS) for automotive, aerospace (AS), civil aircraft (AC), Telecommunications (TL) and Food Safety System Certification (FSSC), just to name a few.

Add to this concepts like World Class Manufacturing, Just-in-Time (JIT), Lean manufacturing, and Six Sigma, and a business owner can feel like they are drowning in alphabet soup.

### Are They Worth It?

Anyone can game a system and there are a significant number of registrars and auditors willing to let a paper system that is seldom utilized or followed pass, as long as the company is willing to pay for the audit. If a company is being pushed by a client and top management believes the system is all smoke and mirrors, it is possible to find a way to get by with a minimum cost and a few days of pain each year when the audits are performed.

However, the external cost of the audit is the same whether the audit is a quick run in, look the other way when a non-conformance is spotted, and hand the company a certificate to slap on the wall, or a real look at the company systems with an objective of improving the system. If both cost the same, why not end up with something useful to the company instead of an expensive wall plaque?

### Real life example

I was director of quality for an automotive supplier. We got ISO 9001 and then TS 16949 certifications, mostly because it was the only way to stay a first tier supplier. Six weeks later we received an order from a new customer for their entire line of vehicles, at list price. We had not quoted or even received a request for quote. We were the only manufacturer of our product with certification so we were automatically added as their approved supplier. Within 2 years we grew from $20 million in sales to $40 million and identified a minimum of $100,000 in annual cost avoidance—driving the savings to bottom line profits.

One of the reasons I find business owners reluctant to implement systems such as ISO is that the owner has been clubbed over the head with the standard by employees for no good reason. The standards are part of business systems, meant to improve the business not create roadblocks to progress. Using, "[the standard] won't let us…" as an excuse is just that, an excuse. Perhaps the equipment is not capable of producing consistently good parts and peoples' bonuses are resting on output, not output minus returns.

Perhaps the employee is having difficulty justifying the rejected production or coming up with a solution. Perhaps the employee thinks they aren't doing a good job unless they reject a certain level of product. Whatever the reason, all the standards allow for a request for concessions from the customer and to re-work product to meet end item specifications. They all also require not only a correction for the specific lot, but an investigation into the cause of the problem and a plan to prevent a reoccurrence in the future. That prevents future waste from scrapped parts or reworked labor.

## ISO 9001

The International Organization for Standardization (ISO) was mostly a European-based group. They created standardization for things like shipping containers and pads of paper. They met annually and asked their members  what they thought should be discussed. It was usually things, not systems.

In the 1980s Japan emerged as a manufacturing leader due to their quality systems. The United States was not far behind although there was some fracturing due to which quality teacher a company followed. European manufacturing was being left behind with higher costs and poorer quality products.

ISO decided they needed a quality system, but how could they make up the years during which the Japanese and Americans had leaped ahead? The recommendation was to utilize a British standard for quality, BS 5750. ISO adopted it verbatim, very proud of their European wisdom, only to find out it was actually a USA Military Standard, MIL-Q-9858 developed during World War II.

At that time it was very difficult to get approval to sell product to the Japanese. They wanted significant testing and documentation that a reliable quality system was in place, and it seemed the seller was hearing a thousand versions of "yes" but no changes in buying habits. The cost and time frame to meet the requirements was exorbitant with little return on investment.

In the USA, each company had their own auditors and system requirements. Companies had to meet multiple standards, provide redundant systems and documents, and stand frequent audits. Companies had to maintain a large auditing staff to visit suppliers.

ISO 9001 provided an answer. The Japanese agreed certification to ISO 9001 would meet their requirements for a supplier. Europe agreed companies certified to ISO 9001 did not have to be inspected for quality. The USA manufacturers realized they could see significant cost reduction by eliminating auditors. Their suppliers reduced costs by eliminating redundant systems, documentation, and audits.

All the way around it seemed like a winning situation, until the automotive companies entered the discussion. They had followed Dr. Deming, a statistician, and had implemented strong requirements for statistical process control (SPC) which they did not want to give up and was not included in the original ISO 9001. The solution became QS 9000 which eventually was replaced with TS 16949. It was the ISO 9001 standard plus additional requirements. Other industries took their cue from the automotive industry and developed similar standards. The auditing was still left to a third party and suppliers still only had to stand a single audit.

Auditors for ISO 9001 must demonstrate proficiency and experience in a business area to audit that sector. So an auditor with only banking experience cannot audit manufacturing unless they can demonstrate substantial experience working in manufacturing as well as banking.

Auditors are trained and tested prior to being registered to audit. They must then work as an auditor under the supervision of an experienced lead auditor and undergo continuing education in the quality field prior to approval to audit independently and eventually to become a lead auditor. Auditors are not allowed to consult. While this was followed much more strictly in the late '80s and '90s, it is still a requirement. The auditor cannot recommend corrective actions to findings. If they were to do so, it would be considered consulting and they could no longer audit your company. Of course, there are ways around the requirements, but I would not recommend them.

### Real life example

Enron was an energy company that used Arthur Anderson to both advise and audit. Enron used loopholes and poor reporting to hide billions of dollars in debts, misleading the board of directors. Some of the Arthur Anderson staff were pressured to ignore issues until the whole house of cards collapsed. It was a classic case of fraud and an example of why auditors should not consult and audit the same client.

ISO 9001 is different from Lean or Six Sigma or even World Class in that it takes into account the entire business system from management through the temporary worker. One of the key lessons of the quality masters was that positive management support is vital to a successful quality management system. It requires good communication and a focus on continuous improvement as a source of business stability.

## ISO 14001

ISO 14001 is an environ-
mental standard, and why
more companies don't adopt
it is an unanswered question.
The standard is very similar to
ISO 9001 and ISO has been
working for decades to make
them so similar they can be

combined for a single audit, reducing audit costs. The concept
behind ISO 14001 is that consumption and waste output should
be continuously reduced to conserve resources. The actual savings from implementing the system can be phenomenal.

ISO 14001 requires companies to identify their consumption and
waste output and then find ways to reduce both but generate
the same production output. If a company can make the same or
more parts with less materials and energy, then the piece price of
the part has to be less. If the amount of waste going to landfills
is reduced, overhead is reduced. In each of these situations, profit
should drive to the bottom line.

## Lean

Lean improves process flow by looking for wastes and finding
ways to increase speed thus reducing process time. It looks at
Just-In-Time (JIT) manufacturing to eliminate inventory carrying costs and for points where non-conforming parts could be
made and how to correct them. The problem solving tools are
frequently considered Lean activities. It works on a pull system
instead of a push system.

In a push system the start of the line determines the line speed
and pushes work as fast as possible to the next station. Unbal-

anced processes create queuing points. Materials are tied up in Work-In-Process (WIP) and if a non-conformance occurs, multiple parts could be affected. A pull system works from demand. The end of production not the beginning determines the speed. As an assembly is completed and packed, the operator at the end of the line pulls the next part from the previous position, which is repeated up the production line. There is no queuing, and balancing issues are easy to identify. Once a line is balanced, in Lean an operator is taken away and a study is performed to see what operations can be eliminated and work redistributed to balance the line.

This is where the industrial engineer could be extremely helpful, but time studies, motion studies, and line balancing are becoming lost arts. Most companies do not keep an industrial engineer on staff, expecting the mechanical engineer to have the skills to design a balanced line. They do not understand that most mechanical engineers have no training in that field.

Time studies involve more than using a stopwatch. A practitioner of Motion-Time-Measurement provides an analytical review. It is rather a different approach from the Lean tool of deliberately unbalancing a line and seeing how the operators fix it. The Lean method stresses operators by forcing them to scramble to be effective. It risks increases in non-conformances.

## Real life example

A client brought me in to build time studies and define the operations in a USA plant. They were looking to see if they could either save by taking the manufacturing off-shore or find ways to reduce labor costs locally. A manufacturing line had four workstations and all the operators were trained and efficient on all the workstations.

The first two were welding operations followed by an extensive wiring operation and packing and palletizing. A single unit was completed every 51 seconds. The first operation took approximately 11 seconds, the second 49 seconds, the third 15 seconds, and the fourth 6 seconds. The fourth position utilized spare time (while waiting for the 51 second operation to be completed) to act as material handler. The operators realized they needed more productivity per man-hour to keep the jobs local, so they would run an operator short with operators one and three using their wait time to do the fourth position and they took turns staggering breaks so the person left behind would work at operation two, stockpiling parts for when the other workers returned. All of these efforts created serious line imbalances and stress on the operators without a significant increase in productivity over the 51 second per unit rate, but they did lower the labor cost.

I was working with a great mechanical engineer. He was able to pull a third welder out of storage, spent $200 for tooling, and we added an operator at the second position doing the same work. Line productivity increased to one unit every 15 seconds.

As the standard was built, the company was paying for 3.40 labor minutes per unit. The operator changes brought this down to 2.55 labor minutes per unit. By balancing the line, we brought the cost down to 1.25 labor minutes per unit—just shy of a 2/3 reduction in standard labor cost per unit.

## Six Sigma

*Statisticians, skip this section: it is written so the average person can understand and contains huge generalizations.*

Six Sigma is focused on reducing process variation. Think bell curves. Sigma is a standard deviation from the norm. It is probability. What are the probabilities that the next part made will vary from the average, and by how much? In normal operations here is how production falls:

- 68% of the parts will be within 1 sigma (standard deviation)
- 95% of the parts will be within 2 sigma
- 99.7% of the parts will be within 3 sigma
- 99.9999998% of parts will be within 6 sigma

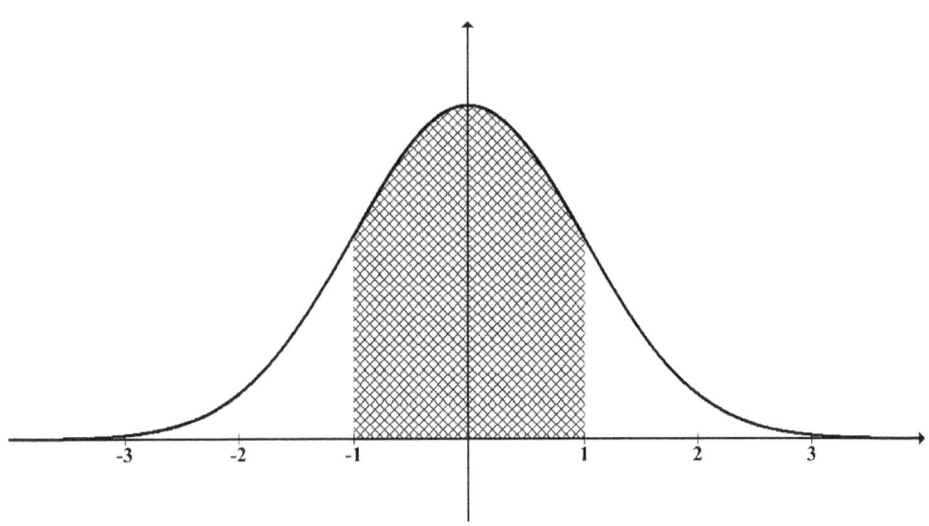

What does this mean to profits?

When the standard distribution is compared to the specification limits the company can predict how much good product will be produced if nothing goes wrong.

If Six Sigma falls within the specification limits, then .0000002% of production or 2 parts in 10,000,000 will not meet the design requirements. In most applications, this means the process is fully capable and does not need to be monitored. Remember back in the first chapter, "Fly Poop in the Pepper," the discussion about not wasting resources measuring if the measurement wasn't re-corded, and not recording the measurement if action wasn't go-ing to be taken? A process capable at Six Sigma isn't going to need action, so measurements don't need to be taken.

**Six Sigma versus Lean versus ISO**
They are not either/or programs, but are complementary. Don't let their special terms and heavy-duty math basis make you skep-tical of implementing them. The tools are simple and easy to use.

**World Class**
World Class is all about implementing best practices. It looks to implement just-in-time, single minute exchange of dies (SMED), cross-functional teams, multi-skilled employees, visual workplace, statistical process control, and total productivity maintenance.

It employs both Lean and Six Sigma. It focuses in on the cost of changeovers and how to reduce them so a changeover takes a minute or less.

### Real life example

A plastic injection molding company started in Germany and developed facilities worldwide. They were very specific on the configuration of the presses down to the smallest detail, as well as the format of the dies. There was a lot of joking in the plants about the top management being this specific and demanding.

An international customer was experiencing huge demand in the USA. Demand was more than double the highest projections, while in Germany demand was slightly below projections. The German demand could be met with a single die and they had two, so one was shipped to the USA plant. Because of the specificity of the top management, the German die was installed in a press and running 100% good parts 15 minutes after being uncrated.

World Class proposes that all operators should be continuously trained so that any operator can perform any operation.

### Real life example

A plant in a small Wisconsin town made several appliances used in homes. The plant was just about the only employer in town, and employees would stay for their entire careers. The appliances were significantly different and very complicated. Each assembly station would take close to 2 minutes, with hundreds of steps. Each employee could perform at or above rate on every position of every appliance. Hunting season was no problem. Summer was a big sales period but productivity did not drop because of the flexibility of the workforce.

World Class utilizes cross-functional teams, total productivity maintenance, and visual work place.

### Real life example

A manufacturer of metal parts had two plants, one in England and one in Yugoslavia. Shortly after world War II they spent their resources to tool the facilities exactly the same and had just brought the production up to 100% of capacity when the Iron Curtain fell. The plant in Yugoslavia was cut off, no tools or equipment could go in. When the Iron Curtain was lifted the company finally got back into their Yugoslavia plant. Management was very skeptical that the plant or equipment would have any level of productivity and they were considering replacing all the equipment in the plant. After all, the plant in the UK had gradually lost productivity as the equipment wore out and was down to 73% of the original production. They were shocked to find the Yugoslavia plant running at 130% of capacity. The plant workers had developed teams to find ways to make the plant more efficient and performed repairs and maintenance to increase the performance of the machines above design specification.

World Class also looks at reliability.

### Real life example

A Japanese manufacturer of industrial building equipment such as earthmovers, bulldozers, etc. wanted to get into the American market but met with significant resistance. Rather than spend resources repeating existing designs they purchased top-of-the-line

American manufactured equipment and reverse engineered it. (My personal opinion is they owed the original manufacturer for the original design.) They realized that was not going to be enough to break into the American market so they took the American machines and drove them until they broke. They analyzed why the part failed, then engineered a superior replacement part. The machines were driven 24/7 and as soon as they failed the engineers swarmed in to figure out how to prevent future failures. They then built their own machines and worked them 24/7. When they had gathered thousands of hours of run time data they went to work selling in the American market with proof that their lower-cost equipment was more reliable.

## Summary

- Lean looks to minimize the cost of the process to produce good parts.
- Six Sigma is looking to control each individual piece of the process so good parts are made every time.
- ISO is looking to make sure management is well organized and communicating to prevent wasting resources.
- ISO 9001 looks at quality from an entire business perspective not just a focus on manufacturing.
- There are a number of industry specific standards which are based on ISO 9001.
- ISO 14001 looks at reducing consumption of resources and production of waste. It can be massively effective at driving profit to the bottom line.
- World Class Manufacturing combines Lean, Six Sigma, and many other tools to increase production and quality.

# Chapter 9

The Old Masters

**Chapter in a Nutshell:**
Who were the quality masters from the 1980's, and how are they the same and different?

Who were Shewhart, Deming, Juran, Crosby, and Taguchi and why should today's business owner care? Weren't they around in the 1980s? That was a long time ago. Hasn't business changed?

Business today has changed, in large part because of the foundation laid by these men in the 1980s. Their systems drove the American war machine during the last world war, and in later years lifted the Japanese manufacturers from ignominy to world leaders in manufacturing. While we have more technology, the principles are the same: treat your suppliers and employees fairly and you have the right to expect the same in return.

Unfortunately Jose Ignacio Lopez arrived on the scene in the 1990s reversing much of the progress the old masters made. Where the old masters believed in cooperation and shared information to create real savings for companies, their suppliers, and their customers, Lopez advocated using the shared information from suppliers to force short-term cost reductions with severe, negative, long-term consequences. If you are in business for the quick, big buck, it is a wonder you read this far. Stop reading now, and go research the Lopez effect. If you have a supplier who was burned with that system, it may not be possible to develop the trust and cooperation needed to move both businesses forward until the next generation appears on the scene.

## Where It All Started

Go back to post–World War II Japan. Japan has almost no natural resources; all materials have to be imported. From 1945 to 1970, "made in Japan" was synonymous with cheap cost and poor quality. Metal toys and cars were made from recycled beer cans. The cars weren't worth importing. But  in the 1970s and early 1980s that changed forever.

Toyota and Nissan shipped in cars to be sold. They came into Europe and the USA on a totally different format than people were used to experiencing. Where in the American auto world there was a base cost to a vehicle and "optional equipment" had to be added, the Japanese cars came in with all the state of the art options. The buyer selection process was pretty much this: pick a color.

The cars were very inexpensive which made it possible for people who would have been unable to purchase a new, reliable vehicle to enter the new car market. Many of these buyers were college students. These vehicles lasted them well into their entry into the job market with little or no maintenance or reliability issues. By the time they were ready for a replacement vehicle their experience and lack of anti-Japanese sentiment made for repeat buyers. The continued low cost, high value experience grew Japanese car manufacturers into a powerful business segment.

How did the Japanese go from building junk to superlative quality? The key came from one Japanese and three American men who changed the face of manufacturing.

## Dr. Walter Shewhart

Dr. Shewhart was a self-taught statistician with a good background in physics and mathematics. He really was the father of statistical quality control. He worked for Bell Telephone, improving their reliability and clarity. When

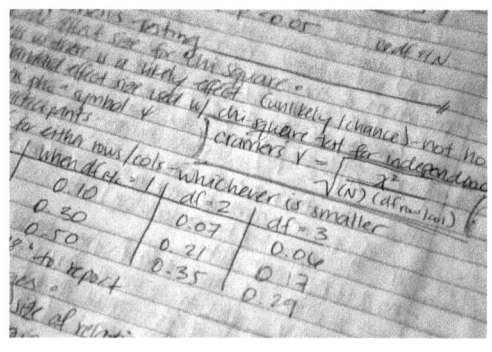

he went to work for Western Electric he sent out a one-page memo that changed control of quality forever. A third of the page was a diagram of a control chart. The remainder of the page laid out the principles that are used today for statistical process control.

He is known for developing the "assignable cause" and "chance cause" variable terms. Assignable cause is when the source of a non-conformance can be identified such as a damaged tool, while chance cause is random and variable and unpredictable. He identified the difference in these causes using mathematical theories applying a normal distribution curve to variations in a manufacturing process.

Unfortunately Shewhart is reputed to have been so steeped in math and science as to not be understood by most people. It took Deming to convert Shewhart's concepts into understandable terms. While Deming is considered by many to be the father of modern day quality systems, it was actually Shewhart who developed the basic concepts.

## Dr. W. Edwards Deming

Dr. Deming was a statistician and a student of Shewhart. While Shewhart was a statistician, he applied his ideas to manufacturing. Deming took the same ideas and applied them to management. During World War II he contributed to the American War Standards. It is no accident that the original MIL-STD used as a basis for ISO 9001 included the concept of leadership of management.

While he tried to teach his concepts in post-World War II America, industry wasn't ready to listen. It was one of those times when short-term profits got in the way of long-term planning. The United States was one of the few manufacturing countries not ravaged by war. People had suffered and conserved, living frugally for the war years, and there was a huge demand for consumer goods. If a company could make it, they could sell it. While statistical process controls had been implemented and used extensively to produce wartime goods, they fell out of favor and were discontinued after the war.

Quality wasn't a big issue. Neither was price. Inefficiencies could be passed on to the consumer, and if it broke there was no longer a need to fix things, just replace them. It was caveat emptor—buyer beware.

Deming went to Japan and told them he would make them successful. He said at the time that no one, even the Japanese, believed him, but he did it.

Here are some quotes from Dr. Deming:

- *The big problems are where people don't realize they have one in the first place.*
- *We are here to make another world.*
- *Declining productivity and quality means your unit production costs stay high but you don't have as much to sell. Your workers don't want to be paid less, so to maintain profits, you increase your prices. That's inflation.*
- *What should be the aim of management? What is their job? Quality is the responsibility of the top people. Its origin is in the boardroom. They are the ones who decide.*
- *All anyone asks for is a chance to work with pride.*
- *If you can't describe what you are doing as a process, you don't know what you're doing.*
- *The prevailing—and foolish—attitude is that a good manager can be a good manager anywhere, with no special knowledge of the production process he's managing. A man with a financial back-*

*ground may know nothing about manufacturing shoes or cars, but he's put in charge anyway.*
- *Any manager can do well in an expanding market.*

Deming was best known for his 14 points, 7 deadly diseases, and his Plan-Do-Check-Act cycle.

## 14 Points[2]

1. Create constancy of purpose for continual improvement of products and service to society, allocating resources to provide for long range needs rather than only short term profitability, with a plan to become competitive, to stay in business, and to provide jobs.
2. Adopt the new philosophy. We are in a new economic age, created in Japan. We can no longer live with commonly accepted levels of delays, mistakes, defective materials, and defective workmanship. Transformation of Western management style is necessary to halt the continued decline of business and industry.
3. Eliminate the need for mass inspection as the way of life to achieve quality by building quality into the product in the first place. Require statistical evidence of built in quality in both manufacturing and purchasing functions.
4. End the practice of awarding business solely on the basis of price tag. Instead require meaningful measures of quality along with price. Reduce the number of suppliers for the same item by eliminating those that do not qualify with statistical and other evidence of quality. The aim is to minimize total cost, not merely initial cost, by minimizing variation. This may be achieved by moving toward a single supplier for any one item, on a long-term relationship of

loyalty and trust. Purchasing managers have a new job, and must learn it.

5.  Improve constantly and forever every process for planning, production, and service. Search continually for problems in order to improve every activity in the company, to improve quality and productivity, and thus to constantly decrease costs. Institute innovation and constant improvement of product, service, and process. It is management's job to work continually on the system (design, incoming materials, maintenance, improvement of machines, supervision, training, retraining).

6.  Institute modern methods of training on the job for all, including management, to make better use of every employee. New skills are required to keep up with changes in materials, methods, product and service design, machinery, techniques, and service.

7.  Adopt and institute leadership aimed at helping people do a better job. The responsibility of managers and supervisors must be changed from sheer numbers to quality. Improvement of quality will automatically improve productivity. Management must ensure that immediate action is taken on reports of inherited defects, maintenance requirements, poor tools, fuzzy operational definitions, and all conditions detrimental to quality.

8.  Encourage effective two-way communication and other means to drive out fear throughout the organization so that everybody may work effectively and more productively for the company.

9.  Break down barriers between departments and staff areas. People in different areas, such as Leasing, Maintenance, and Administration, must work in teams to tackle problems that may be encountered with products or service.

10. Eliminate the use of slogans, posters, and exhortations for the work force, demanding Zero Defects and new levels of productivity, without providing methods. Such exhortations only create adversarial relationships; the bulk of the causes of low quality and low productivity belong to the system, and thus lie beyond the power of the work force.

11. Eliminate work standards that prescribe quotas for the work force and numerical goals for people in management. Substitute aids and helpful leadership in order to achieve continual improvement of quality and productivity.

12. Remove the barriers that rob hourly workers, and people in management, of their right to pride of workmanship. This implies, among other things, abolition of the annual merit rating (appraisal of performance) and of Management by Objective. Again, the responsibility of managers, supervisors, and foremen must be changed from sheer numbers to quality.

13. Institute a vigorous program of education, and encourage self-improvement for everyone. What an organization needs is not just good people; it needs people that are improving with education. Advances in competitive position will have their roots in knowledge.

14. Clearly define top management's permanent commitment to ever improving quality and productivity, and their obligation to implement all of these principles. Indeed, it is not enough that top management commit themselves for life to quality and productivity. They must know what it is that they are committed to—that is, what they must do. Create a structure in top management that will push every day on the preceding 13 Points, and take action in order to accomplish the transformation. Support is not enough: action is required!

## Seven Deadly Diseases[3]

1.  Lack of constancy of purpose
2.  Emphasis on short-term profits
3.  Evaluation by performance, merit rating, or annual review of performance
4.  Mobility of management
5.  Running a company on visible figures alone
6.  Excessive medical costs
7.  Excessive costs of warranty, fueled by lawyers who work for contingency fees

He also listed a lesser category of obstacles
1.  Neglecting long-range planning
2.  Relying on technology to solve problems
3.  Seeking examples to follow rather than developing solutions
4.  Excuses, such as "our problems are different"
5.  The mistaken belief that management skills can be taught in classes
6.  Reliance on quality control departments rather than management, supervisors, managers of purchasing, and production workers
7.  Placing blame on workforces who are only responsible for 15% of mistakes where the system designed by management is responsible for 85% of the unintended consequences
8.  Relying on quality inspection rather than improving product quality

---

3 wikipedia.org/wiki/W._Edwards_Deming

## Plan Do Check Act

Plan Do Check Act is at-
tributed to Dr. Deming but
originally came from Dr. Shewhart. There are a number of
variations as individuals put
their own understanding into
action. Very simply the point
of each step is as follows:

Plan—Set targets goals and objectives. What do you want to accomplish and how will you know when you did accomplish it?
Figure out the steps that need to be accomplished.

Do—Implement the plan.

Check—Did it work? If not, how can it be tweaked or changed
to get it to accomplish the objective? This includes going back
and planning new actions.

Act—Once the check shows the plan worked, implement it. Include in the implementation similar situations and areas where it
would be effective.

If you want to know more about Dr. Deming's concepts and
ideas try reading "Out of Crisis."

## Dr. Joseph Juran

I have to say I have always considered Dr. Juran "a cool dude." He
was an electrical engineer who got a law degree and was admit-
ted to the bar during the depression just in case manufacturing
failed entirely and he needed a new career. Like Shewhart and
Deming, he also worked for Western Electric. He was a prolific
writer and his "Quality Control Handbook" is still as clear and as

effective a guide to quality systems as it was when he first wrote it in 1951.

While Deming worked in Japan focusing on statistical applications, Juran worked on management principles. When he read Vilfredo Pareto's work, which said 20% of the population held 80% of the world's wealth, he tried  applying that to quality issues. This led to his principle of the "vital few" and "trivial many." Juran advocated applying resources to the vital few that would have the most impact in creating change.

Dr. Juran developed the concept of the Quality Trilogy for managing quality. They are:

- quality planning
- quality control
- quality improvement

Dr. Juran focused on the human element and resistance to change. His book "Management Breakthrough" is still applicable. His focus outside the factory to non-manufacturing processes and their contribution to non-conformance costs is different from the other masters of quality.

## Philip Crosby
Mr. Philip Crosby brought quality into terms the average person could understand. His books "Quality is Free" and "Quality Without Tears" were effective, if read. Unfortunately many business owners only read the titles and misinterpreted them.

## Real life example

Back in the 1980s and pre ISO 9001, I was part of a team tasked with selecting the best-fit quality system for a large family-owned and run corporation with roughly 1,000 employees and 5 divisions. The statistical applications of Dr. Deming and Dr. Juran were highly intimidating for top management, but the simple terms used by Philip Crosby were easily understandable. We selected the Crosby system, sending many employees through the Crosby Quality College. It was an effective and useful system that best fit the company culture.

Mr. Crosby's focus was always a top down approach. He proposed 5 ways to assure quality improvement success and 14 steps to establishing process improvement. Many people scoffed at his concept of "zero defects," not understanding it was another method of implementing the need to always strive to improve. He also is known for coining the term "DIRTFT" (dirt-foot) which stands for "do it right the first time."

## 5 Ways to Assure the Success of a Quality Improvement Process

1. Make sure management's commitment to quality improvement is genuine and evident.
2. Keep the quality improvement process serious but fun.
3. Make sure everything in the quality improvement process is positive and handled with respect.
4. Make sure all managers are involved in the quality improvement process.
5. Adapt the quality improvement process to the company and/or location's personality.

## 14 Steps to Establish Process Improvement

1. Management commitment for process improvement
2. Quality improvement team to create process improvement
3. Measurement of process improvement
4. Cost of quality and process improvement
5. Quality awareness as it relates to process improvement
6. Corrective action for process improvement
7. Zero Defects planning
8. Employee education creates process improvement
9. Zero Defects day impact on process improvement
10. Goal setting for process improvement
11. Error cause removal for process improvement
12. Recognition of process improvement efforts
13. Quality councils for process improvement
14. Do it all over again for continuous improvement

## Mr. Genichi Taguchi

Mr. Taguchi developed statistical methods for design improvements of manufactured goods, which have been applied to engineering. Since they apply to engineering, they are typically not well known to companies that exclude design and only build to customer prints and specifications. He made three contributions that were new:

- Design of experiments
- Off-line quality control
- A specific loss function

Mr. Taguchi is most noted for his design of experiments. The system has been criticized. He changed the method of sampling. In addition, his system uses an outer array to take into account environmental factors and the combination of such factors and their impact on variation. His  inner array was controllable factors, the items most people consider when looking at an experiment. Think the main ribs on the fishbone diagram excluding the environment [Mother Nature]. The environment gets the outer array. The problem with the system is that the combination of factors is frequently difficult to resolve. Still, it is a useful tool for engineers.

His off-line quality control relates to eliminating variation in the design stage. He developed a three-stage process that looks at the system design, the conceptual level; the parameters or requirements; and the tolerance design. Taguchi developed the insight that allowed the requirements to be set, taking into account variation in the manufacturing process.

It allowed the design to be more robust and it cost less. Once the parameters are designed, variation is tested measuring performance. A limited number of critical parameters are identified and they are closely controlled, letting parameters having little impact on performance to have more variability.

This reduces manufacturing costs by not setting ridiculously tight requirements that don't matter. Think of the real life example of the railing with the +/- .005" tolerance. To build it to those tolerances would require precise layout, expert workers, and expensive fixturing. Building it to +/- .125" provides a functional product meeting the requirements of the situation at a fraction of the cost. The idea is an application to design of not looking for the fly poop in the pepper.

Overall, Taguchi had some interesting new concepts from the other old masters but they have not been as well received and are not always as intuitive as the work of Deming, Juran, and Crosby.

### The Lopez Effect

Over a decade businesses built a level of trust and mutual respect. They shared information which previously would have been carefully guarded. Suppliers provided innovative ideas to reduce cost and were rewarded with a fair profit, until Lopez came along. He was accused of taking intellectual property from GM to Volkswagen, including parts and factory designs. GM claimed VW saved $450 million in expenses with the information, and eliminated GM's competitive advantage in Europe. VW ended up settling with GM. Lopez was fined in a German court but eventually they dropped the criminal charges. Lopez moved to Spain, which refused to extradite him to the United States.

Lopez advocated using the supplier information, which had been shared, against the suppliers themselves. He demanded they not only reduce their price but that they sell at less than cost. The suppliers reluctantly agreed. They had tied too large a portion of their sales to the big companies where Lopez worked. However, they did get the last word.

When the suppliers protested, pointing out the strides Lopez's company had made using the suppliers' design and development teams, Lopez told the suppliers to put all the development costs into products for their other customers and remove them from his company's price.

Infuriated, the suppliers agreed but decided that since the big company was no longer paying for design, they wouldn't get the improvements they were creating. Instead, they took all the innovations to Lopez's competitors. Within a few years the Lopez led company was so far behind in innovation they lost a double digit percentage of sales.

## Back to the Original Question

Is there value in studying the old masters' concepts? Yes. Is one better than the others? No. They work very well when applied together to best meet the current needs of a company.

## Summary

- The concepts defined by Shewhart, Deming, Juran, Crosby, and Taguchi are just as applicable today as when they were proposed.
- Shewhart started the ball rolling but was hard to understand.

- Deming took Shewhart's statistical methods and applied them to management.
- Juran developed management systems and is known for broadening the application of Pareto's 80/20 rule.
- Crosby wrote up quality systems in a way the average person could understand and advanced the concept of continuous improvement; he said to make it fun.
- Taguchi developed systems for testing in the design stage which allow for the identification of critical parameters and advocated very loose tolerance on parameters which were not critical to minimize manufacturing costs.

# Chapter 10

Blue Light Special

Dr. Deming's fourth point of the fourteen is: "End the practice of awarding business solely on the basis of price tag. Instead require meaningful measures of quality along with price. Reduce the number of suppliers for the same item by eliminating those that do not qualify with statistical and other evidence of quality. The aim is to minimize total cost, not merely initial cost, by minimizing variation. This may be achieved by moving toward a single supplier for any one item, on a long-term relationship of loyalty and trust. Purchasing managers have a new job, and must learn it."

Breaking this down:

- The cheapest price is not always the lowest cost.
- Find suppliers willing to improve their process as well as meet current requirements.
- Minimize variation in supplied parts.
- Develop a long-term relationship with your suppliers. You both need a reasonable profit to stay in business.

**Lowest Price is Not Always Lowest Cost**

Can you trust your supplier? In "Anchors Away" there is a discussion of perceived honesty of offshore suppliers. If your supplier, on-shore or offshore, will not tell you the truth, they will eventually create a significant failure which may put you out of business.

If you sub-contract your manufacturing to them, will they take your design and start making less expensive products to sell in competition with you?

### Real life example

A company had been told repeatedly that labor costs were lower in Mexico. They had a relationship with another company that made a different but similar product line. The supplier made a simple, inexpensive clamp in Mexico while the company made high-end engineered clamps for adverse, high-stress environments in the USA.

The owners of the company decided to get a quote to make their product in Mexico. Instead of going for competitive bids, they went to this supplier, providing not only the plans but also the material and labor costs to manufacture.

The owners were surprised and a little disappointed to find the part cost plus shipping exactly met their current manufacturing costs. but decided to go ahead with subcontracting all their manufacturing. They closed the plant, laid off the workforce, and went to play golf, expecting the same profits.

Within a year their subcontractor had underbid them on all their contracts. They were forced to sell out the few patents they held, receiving a fraction of the true business cost had they sold a year earlier.

Honesty isn't the only issue with awarding business on price alone. Poor supplier quality can be a hidden cost. If your supplier provides good product 100% of the time there is no need for incoming inspection, but if the supplier is not reliable, staff has to be added which costs your company additional salary, benefits, and taxes.

Additionally, even if the product is 100% inspected, 15% of the non-conformances are going to get through. This may create jams in processing, which slows your company's productivity and puts your equipment at risk of damage. What is even worse is if the non-conformances get through and get to your customer. Your company now assumes the risk and potential losses.

### Real life example

A woodworking clamp company made high quality wood and metal clamps. A key customer demanded they also provide a less robust plastic clamp. Knowing this was outside their expertise they contracted offshore for the plastic clamps.

At first they did a direct ship to their customer but quality issues plagued the product and undermined the relationship between the company and the customer. The company tried to work with the supplier with limited success.

Finally, they started having the product brought into their facilities and performing 100% inspection to weed out the non-conforming product. As usual, trying to sort good parts from bad bit them in the rear-end. Non-conformances got through and the clamp company lost their major customer who was 60% of their sales.

In both these cases the company made a decision solely on purchase price and it cost them their businesses.

### Investing in Process Improvement

Your business doesn't stay static. What is acceptable to your customer today is inadequate tomorrow. Your customer is looking for lower piece price, shorter delivery time, and easier service so you should be looking for the same things from your supplier. You are in this venture together in that your continued success ensures your supplier's greater potential for success.

While the automotive industry demands a percentage reduction in price each year of a component's life, it is a pretty adversarial method of working with their suppliers and has some serious drawbacks. If you can partner with a supplier that has a continuous improvement program they will be looking to address reducing their lead-time and piece price to you.

### Real life example

A major supplier of motors to a segment of the automotive industry tried to force a cost reduction by going to their suppliers demanding they re-quote all of their parts. They had three suppliers for each part and let them know who was their bidding competition. They did not want the quotes as simply piece price but each company had to quote materials, labor, overhead, and profit.

The suppliers balked but the threat of being eliminated as a supplier made them reluctantly agree. After receiving the information the motor company selected the lowest labor, material, and overhead across the three different bids. They removed the profit factor and told the suppliers that was the price they would pay for the parts. Every single supplier walked away from the negotiations declining to meet the reduced price. Faced with losing all of their suppliers, the motor company ended the program.

While it is always important to find ways to reduce costs it is just as important to make sure your suppliers are going to be in business for the long term. If they are not investing in process improvements, it should be a concern for their continued viability.

### Real life example

An air filtration company asked for help at becoming ISO 9001 certified. It was a small company of five people. The air filtration company provided the engineering and project management of equipment and subcontracted construction and also the manufacture of proprietary filtration media.

In looking at the management of their supplier for the media, it became very clear the supplier's company was not well run. The company would shut down on days the owner wanted to go fishing, there were no documented procedures, and only the owner knew how to run product correctly. The air filtration company was at significant risk.

We went to the supplier asking for in-process controls, documentation, and other improvements. The supplier refused to make any changes. At this point I strongly recommended the air filtration company look for a new supplier for media. While they were looking for a secondary supplier, disaster happened. Someone other than the owner manufactured a large batch of the media and shipped it direct to the air filtration company's customers. The product had a significant non-conformity. The owner had gone fishing and was unavailable. A qualification run had been scheduled with a new supplier. The air filtration people were on-site and able to give approvals to run re-placement media solving the problem. By looking for a company willing to implement in process controls and improvements the air filtration company stayed in business.

## Minimize Variation in Supplier Parts

In today's world many products are machined complete with a CNC or screw machine or 3-D printed. Variation is in the raw material and it can have significant impact. Polypropylene from two different suppliers will have significantly different responses to the same temperature and pressure. Stainless steel will have slightly different sweeteners from supplier to supplier, which can have an impact on the amount of lubricant and the cutting angle/tool wear. While there will be variation lot to lot, the difference between suppliers will have significantly more impact.

Dr. Deming suggests reducing variation by having only one supplier for a raw material. The problem with this is Murphy's Law—if something can go wrong, it will, and at the worst possible time.

### Real life example

I worked for a plastic injection molder making cosmetic containers. Minimizing color variation part-to-part and batch-to-batch was critical. The supplier of our colors had a fire and the plant burned to the ground. We had a second supplier with formulation to match our batch colors or we would have been importing color from Europe until the supplier got back up and running.

It therefore makes sense to have multiple suppliers but controlling the variation between suppliers is difficult. This is where Taguchi becomes important. Key characteristics must be controlled and the Taguchi method helps identify those characteristics. Think of surfaces of finished parts and formulation of material where variation will impact the process must be controlled. In the case of the polypropylene, specifying pellet size and/or having optimum settings by supplier may be options.

## Develop Long-term Relationships with Suppliers

It is important to have a supplier willing to work with your company to hold specific requirements without charging a premium. This can be difficult for small companies. Sometimes it feels like your company is a flea trying to control the dog it lives on. The point is, your purchaser should spend time developing relationships, not trying to squeeze a quarter of a cent out of the price of a component.

### Real life example

A client needed to update their ISO 9001 certification. When asked for the approved supplier list, that was no problem. It did look a little suspicious that no incoming material had been rejected in the past year, but I put a pin in that concern and asked for their process to qualify new suppliers. That was when the dusty binder came out and old, hand-typed forms appeared. My concern went up another notch.

I asked for evidence of qualifying a supplier to the system and they trotted out a 10-year-old analysis, questionnaire, etc. Everything demonstrated following the procedure but at this point alarm bells started to go off. I asked for a more recent supplier qualification and was told there wasn't any.

They had not added a supplier in a decade. They did have good correspondence on discussing changing parameters and process improvements, but because they had a good relationship there were no problems with variation in materials or rejections impacting the company's production process. The purchasing agent did have some recent quotes from other potential suppliers but the cost difference was negligible. The suppliers could count on the company's business and the company avoided variations.

## Summary

- The cost of materials, parts, and components is more than just the piece price.
- Make sure your suppliers are as committed to continuous improvement as you are.
- Minimize the number of suppliers and be aware of differences to minimize impact on your process.
- Develop long-term relationships with suppliers; it is worth much more then chasing minimal price reductions.

# Chapter 11

Anchors Away

## Chapter in a Nutshell:
Moving manufacturing offshore or back on

## The Cost of Exodus

The first question to ask is, "Is manufacturing in another country right for my company and my customers?" That is not as simple as it sounds. Just because the piece price is less doesn't make it a good decision. You must include all the costs you will incur and add it to the purchase price. What are the obvious costs?

- shipping
- stock holding costs or rush shipments

- customs costs
- communication costs
- training costs
- tooling costs

Then there are the hidden costs:

- Key employee absence due to supplier visits
- One piece flow/ pull system is almost impossible
- Reduced flexibility and responsiveness to sudden customer demand
- Difficulty implementing Six Sigma quality
- Increased rejections by your customer
- Increased distance between engineering and manufacturing inhibiting cross-communication

> **The Cost of Employee Travel**
>
> The cost for airfare and a week's stay at a hotel in Beijing in 2016 is between $1,500-3,000. In addition, there is ground transportation and food costs. Every time an employee travels to China to resolve an issue or check on productivity, it will cost the company $2,000-3500 out of pocket. This does not include the employee's salary or the loss of having them doing their regular jobs. Expect this to be a minimum monthly expense.

- Risk of theft of intellectual properties
- Tarnished reputation from different labor and environmental laws

## Where Oh Where to Manufacture

The first step is to consider where to move your manufacturing. The primary savings is in the labor unless the industry is being propped up by government subsidies. What is the average labor cost in various countries experiencing manufacturing growth? See Figure 1.

From 2006 to 2010 manufacturing in China grew significantly, much of it relocated from the United States.

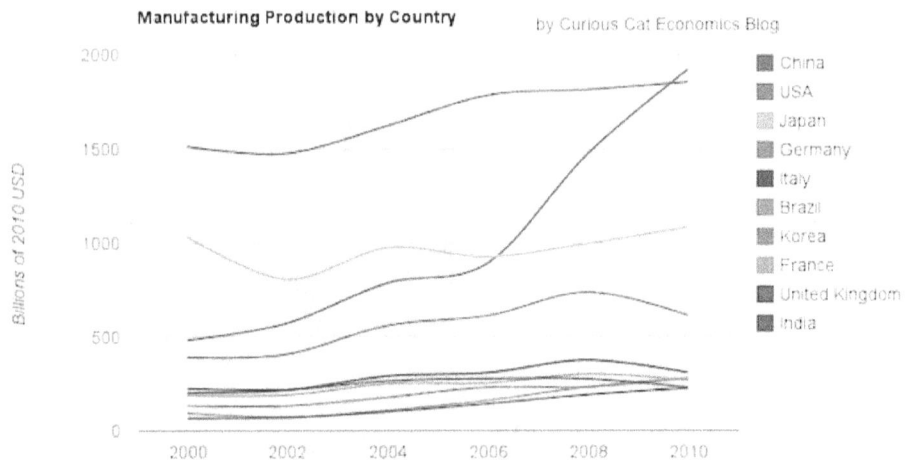

★ chart from http://www.bullfax.com/?q=node-chart-manufacturing-output-2000-2010-country

In Figure 1 the Philippines has the lowest labor rate and a relatively low shipping rate. However, it also has the worst perceived corruption index and a poor air quality index. There is very little data on output per hour. The United States has the 19th lowest labor rate and 7th highest shipping costs out of the 34 rated countries but it has the 3rd highest output per hour, 15th highest perceived honesty rating, and 5th best air quality. As a company owner it is important to consider what this information means to your business.

# Figure 1.

| Country | Hourly compensation and benefits** | Output per hour** $/hr | Perceive *Corruption Index (0-10) | Shipping costs^^ | Air Pollution Rating by WHO^ |
|---|---|---|---|---|---|
| Philippines | $ 2.01 | NA | 2.4 | 660.0 | 47 |
| Mexico | $ 6.48 | NA | 3.1 | 1780.0 | 55 |
| Poland | $ 8.83 | NA | 5.3 | 1025.0 | 33 |
| Hungary | $ 9.17 | NA | 4.7 | 875.0 | 27 |
| Taiwan | $ 9.34 | 139.6 | 5.8 | NA | 98 |
| Estonia | $ 10.39 | NA | 6.5 | 795.0 | 11 |
| Brazil | $ 11.65 | NA | 3.7 | 2275.0 | 40 |
| Slovakia | $ 11.77 | NA | 4.3 | 1540.0 | 27 |
| Portugal | $ 12.91 | NA | 6.0 | 899.0 | 28 |
| Czech Republic | $ 13.13 | 231.7 | 4.6 | 860.0 | 29 |
| Argentina | $ 15.91 | NA | 2.9 | 2260.0 | 38 |
| Korea | $ 18.91 | 183.1 | 5.4 | 695.0 | 61 |
| Israel | $ 21.42 | NA | 6.1 | 565.0 | 59 |
| Greece | $ 21.78 | NA | 3.5 | 1135.0 | 44 |
| Singapore | $ 22.60 | 156.2 | 9.3 | 439.0 | 32 |
| New Zealand | $ 23.38 | NA | 9.3 | 825.0 | 22 |
| Spain | $ 28.44 | 130.6 | 6.1 | 1350.0 | 29 |
| United Kingdom | $ 30.77 | NA | 7.6 | 1045.0 | 23 |
| United States | **$ 35.53** | **155.7** | **7.1** | **1315.0** | **18** |
| Japan | $ 35.71 | 140.4 | 7.8 | 970.0 | 22 |
| Italy | $ 36.17 | 107.3 | 3.9 | 1145.0 | 37 |
| Canada | $ 36.56 | 110.6 | 8.9 | 1660.0 | 13 |
| Ireland | $ 39.83 | NA | 8.0 | 1121.0 | 15 |
| France | $ 42.12 | 125.1 | 6.8 | 1248.0 | 27 |
| Netherlands | $ 42.26 | 131.0 | 8.8 | 975.0 | 26 |
| Austria | $ 43.16 | NA | 7.9 | 1155.0 | 25 |
| Finland | $ 44.14 | 128.9 | 9.2 | 620.0 | 19 |
| Australia | $ 46.29 | 107.5 | 8.7 | 1120.0 | 13 |
| Germany | $ 47.38 | 120.2 | 7.9 | 937.0 | 25 |
| Sweden | $ 49.12 | 148.7 | 9.2 | 735.0 | 25 |
| Denmark | $ 51.67 | 128.1 | 9.3 | 603.0 | 27 |
| Belgium | $ 54.77 | 113.4 | 7.1 | 1400.0 | 26 |
| Switzerland | $ 60.40 | NA | 8.7 | 1440.0 | 22 |
| Norway | $ 64.15 | 124.4 | 8.6 | 1100.0 | 22 |

★ www.economywatch.com 2010 data 0=corrupt, 10= no corruption

★★ftp.bls.gov US Bureau of Labor and Statistics

^ http://www.statisticbrain.com/countries-ranked-by-air-pollution/ Oct 15, 2012 PM10 Air Quality Index ug/m3

^^ http://search.worldbank.org/data?qterm=cost%20to%20import&language=EN cost for shipping a 20 ft container in 2012

In 2008, baby formula shipped from China was found to contain Aflatoxin and toys were coated with lead-based paint. Pet food contained poisonous wheat gluten, and defective tire stems from China caused dangerous tire failures. Nike faced a severe out-cry about the child labor utilized to make their products and had to launch an expensive campaign to clean up their image. Pilots flying into Beijing say the air is so thick it is like flying through a bowl of milk.

A client is a manufacturer of a consumer home improvement product. One of their engineers spotted a competitor's product on the shelf and bought it to do a comparison. What he found was their product had been duplicated right down to the UL and patent labels. The producer was in a foreign country. The competitor had not contacted UL and of course they did not hold the patent, but the US company was not able to recoup any funds. Due to the

## Manufacturing Management

A long-standing question in social science is the extent to which differences in management cause differences in firm performance. To investigate this we ran a management field experiment on large Indian textile firms. We provided free consulting on modern management practices to a randomly chosen set of treatment plants and compared their performance to the control plants. We find that adopting modern management practices had three main effects. First, it raised average productivity by 11%, through improved quality and efficiency and reduced inventory. Second, it increased the decentralization of decision making, as the better flow of information enabled owners to delegate more decisions to middle managers. Third, it increased the use of computers, necessitated by the data collection and analysis involved in modern management. Since these practices were profitable this raises the question of why firms had not adopted these before. Our results suggest that informational barriers were a primary factor in explaining this lack of adoption. Modern management is a technology that diffuses slowly between firms, with many Indian firms unaware of its existence or impact. And since competition was limited by constraints on firm entry and growth, badly managed firms were not rapidly driven from the market.

1 "Does Management Matter? Evidence From India" by Nicholas Bloom, Benn Eifert, Aprajit Mahajan, David McKenzie, and John Roberts

lax patent laws where the counterfeit product was being made they had no recourse. They did notify the retailers but they have been slow to move away from the foreign supplier.

Another client has their consumer goods manufactured in China. Their products are not patented. What they have found is their competitors make contact with the vendors and buy the same products, selling at a lower cost because they do not have to pay for a staff of designer engineers.

How do you manage long distance suppliers and prevent these kinds of issues?

### "We're Not in Kansas Anymore, Toto"
Treating any supplier from a different country the same as the factory around the corner is the first mistake. There are basic cultural differences. They are not bad. They are not good. They are different.

People work from their frame of reference made up of experience, education, beliefs, and culture. Only when there is a shared frame of reference can there be clear communication. For Nike there was the assumption that adults would manufacture their product. Child labor is a fact of life for the manufacturing companies in many foreign nations and not a cause for concern. Both were acting from two different frames of reference so there was no communication on the subject. Expect to have to specify everything, not just the product.

### Contracts
In one country a contract may be interpreted as a guideline defining the intent and in another the contract does not go beyond the edge of the paper. For example, a chair is ordered with four

casters boxed separately. The intent is that the casters fit onto the chair legs, making it roll. Unless the shaft of the caster and the hole diameter are specified, expect to have issues with the casters either not inserting or falling out.

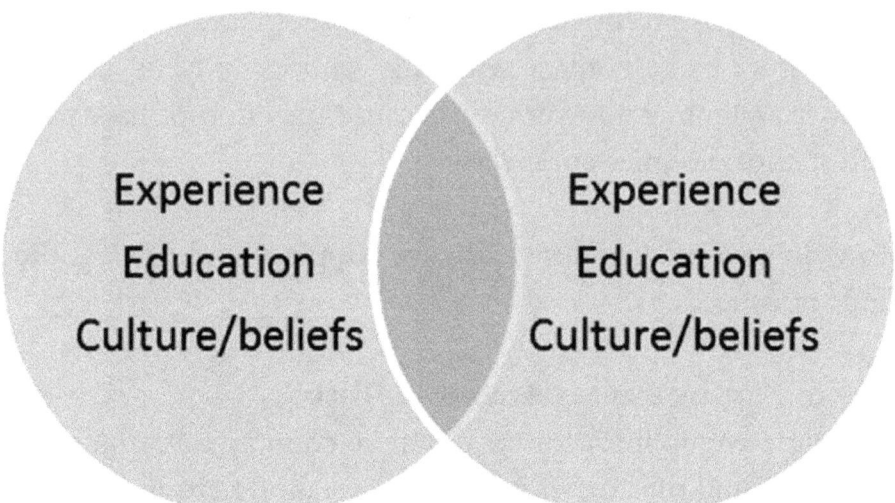

### On-time Delivery

Don't assume the supplier factory will be open just because your company is taking orders. Summers in Europe are for holiday and production slows. Product ordered from France in August may take twice as long to receive as the same order placed in May. If the supplier is in the Far East, be aware that Chinese New Year is going to affect when or even if your product gets loaded onto a boat. Quoted lead times vary throughout the year. Have the supplier identify when the plant is closed.

## Be a Control Freak

### Specifications Are Your Friend

Expect to specify everything. Every dimension and every material must be defined. The exact shade of a color must be specified unless you can accept pink through orange for "red." Every screw, nut, and bolt must be specified with length, material, head shape, and thread type. The company contracting out its manufacturing must have done the interference fit studies on all mating parts. Material substitutions must either be clearly specified or forbidden. Random inspections of the supplier will be a reality and must be in the contracts. In many countries, just because it is in the contract does not mean that is what must be delivered.

## Murphy's Law or FMEA

A complete Failure Mode and Effect Analysis (FMEA) must be performed on each element of the product and each assembly. Assume Murphy's Law: what can go wrong, will go wrong, and at the worst possible time. What will be the impact of that failure? Before the product is put to use, how easy is it to spot the defect? Generally, the more variation the prints allow within the specification, the lower the price. However, it is important that the studies of worst-case scenarios are completed before contracting out the manufacturing.

## Process Control

Visit the factory where the product will be made. Understand the process for each part being manufactured. Perform a complete FMEA on the process. Identify control points and define what controls you require. Perform a process capability study on key operations (the FMEA will tell you which ones). Understand outside of Japan, Europe, and North America, quality is still inspected into the product; defects are not prevented but sorted out and reworked. Rule of thumb: Any human inspection is about 85% effective, so if the process capability says the process is out of control, then defects will get shipped. Can your company survive the customer getting rejects?

## Trust Is Earned

Once the control points are determined, require the supplier to send the process charts for your approval prior to shipment. Review the charts. Compare the new chart to the last one you received. Suppliers have been known to send copies of the same manufacturing chart repeatedly even though the material being shipped was from a different production lot or time period.

Specify that the process cannot be changed without your approval. That must include equipment changes. Different equipment will have different process capabilities and impact the validity of the control charts.

The amount of manual labor involved in the process may require control of personnel to maintain quality. How does your supplier ensure the people making your product are knowledgeable about the process? If the process is

### The Make it in America Challenge

This FFO announces the availability of funding for the Make it in America Challenge. The Make it in America Challenge will provide up to $40 million in competitive grant funding through the DOC's EDA and NIST Manufacturing Extension Partnership (NIST MEP), DOL's ETA, and the DRA. This collaboration allows applicants to submit one application to leverage complementary Federal funding sources to support the development and implementation of a regionally driven economic development strategy that accelerates job creation by encouraging re-shoring of productive activity by U.S. firms, fostering increased Foreign Direct Investment, encouraging U.S. companies to keep or expand their businesses—and jobs—in the United States, and training local workers to meet the needs of those businesses. Federal support for the Make it in America Challenge is expected to be used to fund up to 15 projects, each with a project period of up to 3 years. If, however, a project includes EDA-funded construction, that component of the project may have a project period of up to five years. The funding level of each participating Federal Agency will vary, subject to the availability of their respective appropriations. See Section III, Award Information, in the Full Announcement Text of this FFO.

See the Make it in America Website http://manufacturing.gov/make_it_in_america.html

people-dependent, the question must be asked or the risk is a non-conforming product that upsets your customer.

Don't assume your materials specification will be followed. Require certifications of the materials used. Randomly test the finished product to see if it meets the material specifications.

## Plan for Failure

It is very difficult to think of everything that could fail and cultural differences can lead to unexpected failures. What happens if non-conforming product gets to your customer? Is it possible to recall a specific batch or lot? What is your traceability both out to the customer base and back through the supply chain? How likely are you to get a product liability claim if you can't recall the affected product? If you don't have forward traceability, how likely are you to have to recall all of a product back? What kind of compensation are your customers going to expect?

Suppose there is no product problem but a situation creates a negative public image. How quickly can you launch a campaign to repair public perception?

## Bringing Production Back Home

There has been a gradual up-tick in the number of companies that have decided the benefits of foreign manufacturing are no longer justified. They must decide how to bring the product back on-shore. Usually they start by finding local manufacturers with the plan to continue to contract out the manufacturing process. This eliminates a large capital investment to rent or purchase facilities and purchase equipment and develop internal infra-structure. The first thing that happens is a serious case of "sticker-shock" on the piece price.

## Ask Why

If production has gone offshore why is consideration being given to bring it home? If the reason is government or customer incentives, adjust the manufacturing costs so there is a fair comparison. If the reason for the re-location of manufacturing is a problem, can the problem be resolved at the current facility? Apply root cause analysis to determine if a solution at the current facility is possible.

If the supplier is violating the contracts and trust, knowingly sending inferior or non-conforming product, if supporting the distant facility is having a negative overall impact or the customer requires rapid response, then the best answer is to bring the product into a more easily controlled environment. This usually means bringing it closer to your facility.

## Piece Part Cost

Labor in North America is going to be higher than in the Philippines or China (Figure 1). To get a realistic view of the total cost requires an analysis of total expenses. Converting normal shipping costs into per piece price should be a fairly straightforward exercise. Track rush shipments and see if they relate to a specific part, family of parts, or customer. If possible, assign them to the appropriate parts rather than as an overall average. Check customs documentation and handling costs. How much is being spent on telephone and video communications? How much is being spent on employee travel? Assign the costs appropriately so you have the total cost per piece for your comparison.

## All or Nothing

Many people view manufacturing on- or off-shore as an all or nothing proposition, which may not be the best viewpoint to take. Rush shipments should follow the 80/20 rule (Pareto). Either 20% of the product or 20% of the customers will consume 80% of the rush shipment costs. Can this portion of production be brought closer to home?

Tooling may impact this decision. For example, if a family of parts is manufactured in the same mold with different inserts but only one product results in rush shipments, then the cost comparison has to take into account the whole line. Start with these products and begin shopping for a manufacturer close to home.

## Working with Local Suppliers

Manufacturing in the United States tends to be much more automated than in locations where labor is inexpensive. The purchase of tooling and equipment can make the re-shoring of manufacturing cost prohibitive. To address this, the federal government has set aside $40 million specifically to help encourage re-shoring. Search Grants.gov/Find Grant Opportunities/Opportunity Synopsis

Local suppliers may also be willing to adjust pricing slightly to help absorb overhead. They may be able to negotiate lower material costs depending on your contract terms. Look beyond piece price to see if there is a way to negotiate a position that will satisfy your company's needs and not leave the supplier working at a loss.

Also recognize higher mechanization also results in lower variation. There may be additional economic improvements in your own process.

## Summary

- Moving manufacturing off shore is much more complicated than simply lower labor or piece price.
- Don't assume North-American/European culture and standards.
- Prepare for the risk.
- There are a number of hidden costs in off-shore manufacturing.
- Returning manufacturing from off-shore takes planning and analysis.

# Chapter 12

Gold Watch

**Chapter in a Nutshell:**
Treat employees as a
resource to reduce costs.

A generation ago people went to work for a company and stayed for 20-30 years. When they retired there was a party and the retiree received a gold watch. By 1983 the average worker stayed 3.5 years. In 2012 this had gone up to 4.6 years because of economic issues, not because the employees necessarily wanted to be there.

The economy does influence longevity. Employees tend to stay in jobs longer in a weak economy than in a strong one. Part of this is because fewer jobs are available, and part is from fear. This kind of long-term employee is not much better than when you have a high turnover rate. They are not staying because they are inspired. These employees are staying because they need a pay-check. They are not motivated or interested in what is happening with the company, so while the company gets attendance, it also gets the minimum input and innovation.

No matter what the economy is doing, it is very common for employees to grumble over the difference in wages between the boss and the line workers. Much of this is due to a lack of un-derstanding, which comes from a lack of communication. The employee seldom knows the risks the boss is taking to keep the company in business, or the times the boss doesn't get a paycheck when they do.

The rule of thumb in business is not to let your opponent know where you are vulner-able and many business own-ers view the employees as an enemy, especially if there is a strong union.

### Real life example
During the Stanley Cup playoffs, hockey teams will report a player is injured but not what the injury is so the opponents can't take advantage of the injured player's weakness.

This is a balancing act for the company owner as well. They need to be open with the employees regarding the risks they are tak-ing. The company books don't need to be open or the employees see a copy of the employer's income tax return, but it is important the employees feel the company is going to remain in existence. They also need to know that profits and/or sales are up or down. They need to know the boss is feeling the same "pinch"

they are. It is promoting the idea that "we are in this together" instead of the company and the employees lining up on opposite sides in a tug of war over money.

Dr. Deming was very concerned with the employee-employer relationship. He advocated a "we are in this together" attitude rather than an adversarial approach.

> *Encourage effective two-way communication and other means to drive out fear throughout the organization so that everybody may work effectively and more productively for the company.*

Studies show that 54% of workers like the people they work with but only 29% feel valued.[4] If an employee feels they are not making a difference, they have no reason to be loyal and they might as well go someplace that will pay them more. When they are told repeatedly, "Put your hand in a bucket of water then pull it out. The hole you leave is how much difference you make to this company," there isn't much reason to stay.

---

4 http://www.marketwatch.com/story/americans-less-likely-to-change-jobs-now-than-in-1980s-2014-01-10

In the United States, workers are not considered a resource. Employees, with few exceptions, are considered expendable. This is a mistake.

If you communicate a problem a customer has with a product to the employees involved in manufacturing it and return months later, you will find the employees are watching for and may be instituting extra checks on their time to make sure that problem is not repeated. People, in general, want to do a good job. People, in general, want to hear, "you matter."

### Real life example

An earlier example was a rollform part with the wrong angle. The rollform tooling was corrected so the problem was resolved. However, the employees would always check the angle on an optical comparator at start up to make sure the customer would get good parts. They wanted to be sure old tooling had not been installed accidentally. Even though this company's management had a quasi-adversarial relationship with the employees, the employees said, "no defects on my watch."

## Creating Employees as a Resource

People have to be paid a living wage. If your employees are part of the working poor, don't expect loyalty. If another company offers them a few cents more an hour, they are going to take it out of desperation. No matter how many team building and motivational efforts the company creates, no matter how

much the employee feels they are important to the company, the first requirement of every employee is to provide food, clothing, and shelter for themselves and their families. Look at what your employees are earning relative to the cost of living. Make sure they are not part of the working poor. If they are, don't spend resources on speakers and picnics; move it to the paychecks for a better return on your investment.

If the entry-level position at your company is in the working poor category, there will be a significant level of attrition. Some business owners have rationalized that high attrition is due to a poorly prepared labor pool. Attrition is a process to weed out those who can from those who can't early on. The business own-er owes it to themselves and their company to collect exit data and determine what is the real issue.

Recruiting is expensive. The company is still going to expend funds to review applications and do background checks. It is more cost effective to have as little attrition as possible. If you are getting high entry-level turnover, check to see if the problem is a low entry wage or poor preparation of the employee for the workplace.

Some employees may stay in a low-paying entry position if there is a possibility of wage increases relative to training programs/ increased skill levels and the ability to swiftly move up to a living wage. Be warned, people aren't willing to struggle to survive for long. Those with the skills and determination, the best potential to grow with the company, are going to leave within a few months if they don't see a path for improvement in salary.

If the issue really is a poorly prepared pool of workers, investigate the possibility of setting up a program with a local school or training facility. Give them a view into your needs and let their counselors do the initial work training and qualifying new people.

### Real life example

In the 1990s Lake Zurich, IL High School established a program with local companies. The high school recognized not all students would go on to college. They partnered with local businesses to tailor training and education of students so they could be successful in the local job market. The school made a guarantee: if the company hired a student who did not meet the minimum requirements, the school would provide free training and education to get the student to the minimum level. The employers were confident of getting good candidates for entry positions, the students were prepared and able to be successful, and the school could claim outstanding success in educational preparation.

One of the frustrations I hear from business owners is the employees' expectation of an annual raise. In poor economic periods the business will see a decrease in profits but the employees still want a raise. Consider tying raises to skill levels. Each time an employee increases their skill level they get a raise. The increased skills must be of benefit to the company so a strong training program must exist. Illinois has a state program to assist companies and subsidize a portion of the training costs. The Manufacturing Alliance can help develop grant requests. The state is very slow to pay, about a year in arrears, but the program is one of the few all the politicians agree is of value.

### Real life example

A company had several cells to manufacture goods with multiple stations in each cell. Each cell was a different product line with fluctuating volumes on a seasonal basis. Entry-level employees learned a single position on a single cell. As they learned the other cell positions they saw slight increases in wages. When they could do all the positions on a single cell, they saw a bump in salary. When they learned a position on a second cell they again saw a slight bump. Every time they learned all the positions on a new cell they had another bump.

The company had significant flexibility and was able to function with lower labor staffing through this system. The employees were in control of their raises and felt valued.

## Temporary Labor

Using temporary labor is another option. A number of companies work with temporary agencies to cover seasonal or economic fluctuations. This does give company employees confidence they have a buffer against layoffs. The agency does the recruiting and background checks.

There is a negative side to using temporary agencies. There is no guarantee the company will get the same temporary employee on a repetitive basis. Temps are usually people trying to cover their bills while looking for permanent work. The agency has little control over keeping people so the company can incur basic training costs day after day. Many of these agencies pay very low wages so the employees work for multiple agencies and end up working two full time jobs. This reduces their efficiency and effectiveness—don't be surprised to find a temporary employee asleep at a workstation. If the temporary employee is worth hiring, expect to pay the agency much more than your company would have spent for background checks and recruitment.

## White Collar Employees

Motivating white collar workers can be done similarly to paying employees for increased skills. Have each employee draw up a career path they would like to take. Review and establish milestones and the impact of the career

path on the company. The employee must be aware they have a responsibility to make the company profitable while advancing their own agenda. Set points where salaries will be re-evaluated. If the plan is something that does not benefit the company, explain why it is not going to result in increased wages and recommend mutually beneficial paths. Make the employees as responsible for their success as the company. And demonstrate a link between the company being successful and the employee's potential for success.

## Layoffs

Layoffs can happen. Building a flexible work force is a good buffer against volume fluctuations. Wherever possible, try to address the reduced workforce with attrition. If that is not possible this is one place you don't eat the elephant one bite at a time. Take a long hard look at your market and make all the cuts you will need for the next six months to a year using overtime and temporary labor if needed to fill gaps.

When layoffs happen fear blooms. Employees wonder if they will be next and people with advanced skills tend to look for a new place to work.

As soon as the layoff occurs, bring everyone together. Tell them why the layoff happened and why they don't have to worry that they are next.

### Real life example

An electronic component manufacturer was in a slow decline. At the end of each month for three years there was a layoff, by seniority, to a point where people with 15-20 years of experience with the company were next on the chopping block. Everyone feared they would walk in some morning and find the doors chained shut. Good employees quickly left. People closing in on retirement prayed the company would stay open long enough for them to get Social Security. No one brought up new ideas or improvements out of fear they would be noticed and fired. Eventually the company closed because no one dared change the downward spiral.

## Too Adversarial to Work

Sometimes the relationship between management and the employees has so deteriorated there is no recovery. This should be a rare occurrence. If it is the situation your company is in, management must determine how they got there and then add this analysis to the evaluation for extensive automation investments or move the manufacturing operations.

### Real life example

In the 1960s General Electric had an opportunity for a large contract related to the space program. One key point was a need for rapid and consistent production. Management recognized they could not afford a strike. When the union presented their demands, General Electric agreed to all of them in the first bargaining session. The union was incensed and went on strike because they felt management had failed to negotiate in good faith. They considered it an effort on the part of General Electric to break the union. Eventually the strike was settled. GE was able to meet the contract but immediately developed a plan to move the program from Syracuse, NY to their other plants and never return. Thousands of jobs were lost, permanently.

## Union Shops

What was the cause of the issue with General Electric? Possibly poor communications. Certainly, the automotive industry typically has an adversarial relationship with the union but they were able to successfully implement Dr. Deming's systems in a highly unionized environment.

Having a union in place does not make it impossible to create a positive work environment that benefits the company. Typically the reason a union exists is caused by a lack of trust and understanding between management and the employees. Working on the basis that one "gosh-darn" wipes out a thousand "attaboys," it is time to take an honest look at why a union got started in the first place. It will take significant work and openness on the part of management to change the work environment. There will be push back at first, perhaps for years, and there must be an awareness of individuals' concerns over loss of influence and a fear management is trying to break the union. The union's purpose is to protect the employees from management's manipulation whether the manipulations exist or not. When looking to make a change, the company must approach the union with concrete plans and information as to how the changes will benefit the union and the employees they represent.

Having a union is not always a negative for a company.

> **Real life example**
> The workers at a steel forming shop were represented by an electrical union. On a consistent basis, management would put together their planned amounts for raises, only to have the union demand wages much lower than management planned on giving. The same thing happened at a pharmaceutical company. Their employees were non-union except for a small segment of machinists. The non-union employees got higher raises than the machinists because the company had to abide by the contract.

## Summary:

- Employees are a resource not a disposable commodity.
- Communication of how the employee is being treated relative to management is key to building trust.
- Work to eliminate adversarial relationships between the company and the employees.
- Never do multiple layoffs in close succession.
- If an adversarial relationship exists between employees and management it will take more work to fix it than it would have taken to prevent it.
- Unions are not always a bad thing for the company.

# Chapter 13

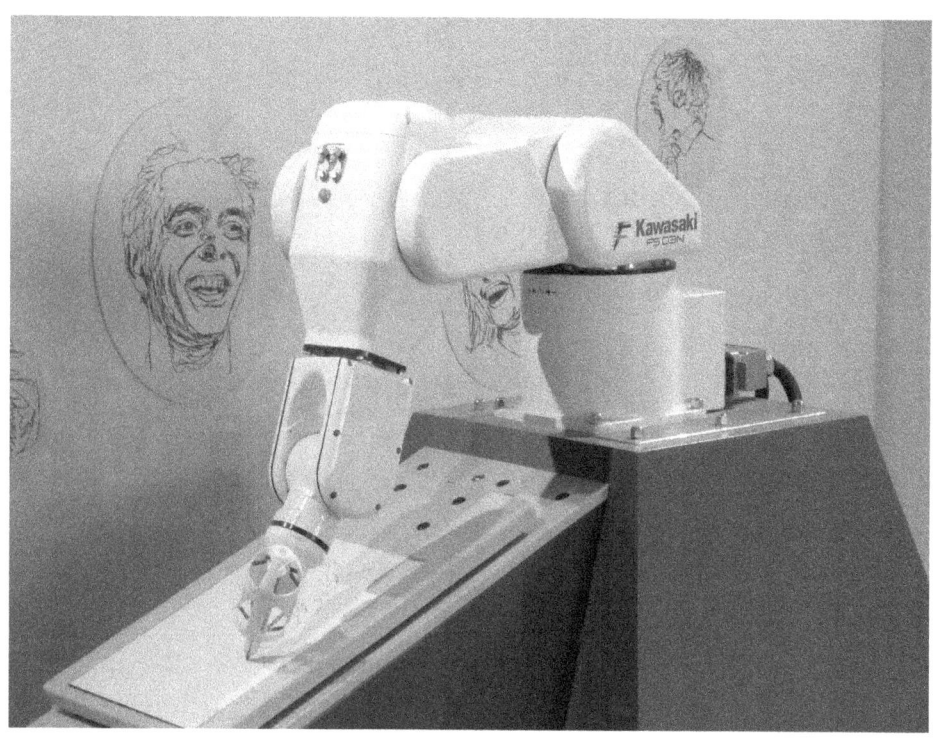

Robbie the Robot

**Chapter in a Nutshell:**
The types of automation projects and how to plan and pay for them.

Automation is a case of pay me now or pay me later. There is a high initial cost, which is paid back in lower salary costs and greater repeatability/quality if done correctly. Maybe.

## The Initial Investment

The initial investment into automating a process is significant. The company can invest in a one-of-a-kind specially designed machine or an assembly of proven component machines or an existing machine in use in multiple industries. Typically the most expensive method is a specially designed machine and the least expensive is an off-the-shelf design. However, both require significant capital investment.

## Banks

The most straightforward method is to go to your bank for a loan. The chances of the company getting a loan are much better for an off-the-shelf machine or standardized components. The bank must always consider how risky the investment is, and what will happen if it fails to achieve its

promises. A one-of-a-kind specialty machine has little opportunity to be easily sold. The chances of selling the machine to recoup the loan are small. This makes it a high risk. The company will generally have to pledge other assets and/or pay a higher interest rate if they can even get a bank to consider the purchase. Off-the-shelf machines or components are easier to sell so most banks will be more willing to make a loan.

### Real life example

An engineered clamp company decided to automate the manufacture of one of their product lines. The projected changes reduced manning from five operators down to one, increased consistency in critical areas, and doubled the volume that could be produced. They went with a specially designed one-of-a-kind machine with each workstation designed and built from scratch. The purchase price was over $2 million, about 5% of sales. The bank loaned them the funds. The project took twice as long as planned to design and build. When it came time to qualify it, the machine volume was less than the original production line and still required two to three operators. The system was very sensitive to variation so there were significant non-conformances at each workstation on a regular basis. After two years, the machine finally ran at 80% of promised speed with two operators and consistent product quality.

### Real life example

A large volume cosmetics firm had a hair care line that accounted for over $1 billion in sales per year. In order to maintain costs and meet demand, the company automated the entire process from batching through boxing, palletizing, picking, and loading shipments. By the time they finished the products were made with a total of seven employees and the equipment ran 24/7/365. It was a tremendous success.

## Grants

Another source of investment capital is grants, usually from governments. While they will be more open to a specially designed machine, government funds are limited, slow to be delivered, and difficult to get. Your bank should be able to assist you in applying for the grant but there is significant competition for limited funds.

## Automation versus Offshore

A company looking to reduce its labor costs can either automate or find less expensive labor. This is usually offshore in a third-world country. As discussed in "Anchors Away," the risks are

significant in going offshore.
Proprietary formulations and
product designs are at risk of
being stolen, and lead-times
are extensive as are shipping
costs. Most countries where
industrialization is just beginning to occur see steadi-
ly rising labor rates so by the time production is stabilized and
meeting the customer requirements the labor cost will be ap-
proaching that of the USA. And there are risks of poor quality
materials, contaminated materials, and manufacture with child or
slave labor. The one advantage is a smaller initial investment than
automation.

When properly done, automation reduces variation from piece
to piece. If the product is made to sell to consumers, reduced
variation can reduce risk and increase customer satisfaction. If
the product is a component, and is sold to another business, the
reduced variation is a significant sales feature. Highly automated
processes do not generally see annual increases in cost beyond
those experienced from the raw material. Automated systems
generally produce at a faster rate allowing for shorter lead-times.
Automation should always be evaluated for the time to change
over. Long changeover times can force the use of economic order
quantities, which equates to a high cost for carrying inventory.

**Operator Requirements**
One issue with automation is the need for highly trained operators. This is not a position that can be performed by a temporary operator. The operator needs to be knowledgeable about the
product requirements, historical issues, the machine performance
and maintenance needs, as well as aware of issues with inputs to

the system that could damage the equipment. There is a significant investment in training the employee. If this is on a one-of-a-kind machine, the skill set is not easily transferable, but if it is a known off-the-shelf system, training opens avenues for the operator to move to a different company.

## Ordering and Accepting

A key point in ordering either an off-the-shelf or one-of-a-kind automation is understanding and agreement on requirements by both the manufacturer of the machine and the company purchasing the machine. The inputs to the system and the requirements of the system output must be clearly defined. Those outputs include both quantity and quality. Reliability and maximum downtime for maintenance should be included. Maximum changeover times and the range of variation in the product must be defined. A good tool for measuring if the project was completed satisfactorily is a Production Part Approval Process (PPAP), developed by the Automotive Industry Action Group (AIAG). These documents are available online and are designed to confirm a process is capable of supplying a consistent product reliably.

## Real life example

I was called in at the end of an automation project. The client wanted a power cord attached to the assembly but did not tell the company designing the line automation. I was given the task of designing that portion of the line in a 5 ft x 10 ft area with a maximum of two operators. When I gave them the completed design the client mentioned two labels had to be attached to the cord at this position too, and they wanted the station manned with only one operator. When the client was told this would require a redesign of the machine they decided not to go forward with the project as they had run out of time to implement it. Everyone walked away from that project unhappy because of changing requirements.

## Summary

- The biggest challenge to automating a process is the large investment.
- Off-the-shelf versus one-of-a-kind automation projects have different likelihoods of being funded and achieving success.
- Automation should be considered and compared to moving manufacturing off shore.
- Automation requires higher skilled operators.
- The project must be clearly defined at the start to be successful.

# Chapter 14

Getting Better and Better

**Chapter in a Nutshell:**
Continuous improvement is a must, so what is best for your company?

Either the company gets better at what it does or it falls behind and eventually goes out of business, so it is important to have a continuous improvement program. There are many such programs out there.

Continuous improvement is different from fixing problems and implementing prevention. Continuous improvement looks specifically for ways to cut time and costs out of the process without negatively impacting quality.

Here are a few continuous improvement tools.

## Lean and Six Sigma

The two most common programs are Lean and Six Sigma which were discussed in Chapter 8, "Alphabet Soup." They are good tools as long as they remain tools to improve the company toward increased sales or increased profit. It is easy to get so lost in their implementation that they become an end instead of a means to an end.

## World Class Manufacturing

A more detailed in-depth tool is World Class Manufacturing. It uses best practices and encourages developing new practices to optimize manufacturing. It addresses reducing set up times, creating cellular manufacturing, reducing work in process (WIP), reducing variation, and focusing on the vital few and not the trivial many. It utilizes Just In Time and Lean, and implements a total quality management systems and total productivity maintenance.

## Critical Path Scheduling

The Critical Path Method (CPM) is a basic industrial engineering technique for planning, scheduling, and controlling projects. It started out on paper but is now typically automated. It looks for the fastest path through a process, the order processes need to be completed in, what processes can be done simultaneously, and which must be done in series.

Typically only 5% of the activities are on a critical timeline. The remaining 95% of the activities can be completed in less time than a simultaneous critical activity. Once the constraining path is identified projects can be implemented to reduce the time for each of those steps, reducing the overall time of the project.

# Example

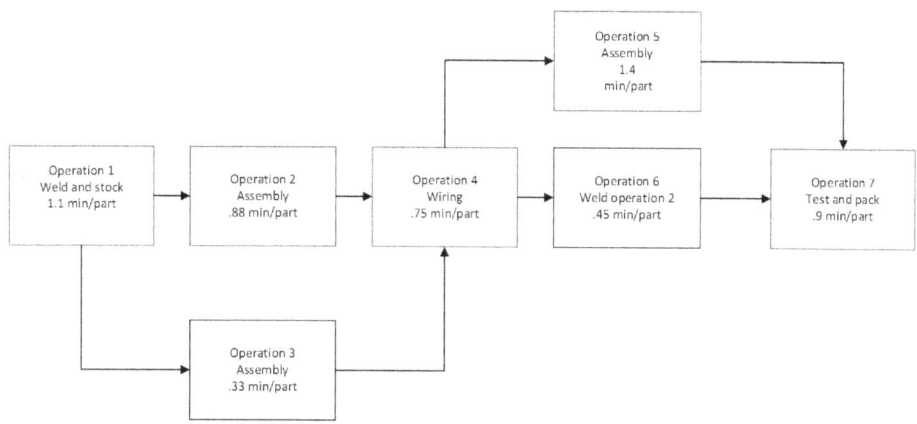

This is a simple project. The critical path is red, non-critical items are black. In this particular case, the critical operation is the second welder, Operation 5, followed by the first welder, Operation 1. The maximum through-put of this line is 1 part every 1.4 minutes or about 42 parts per hour. CPM tells us what is obvious from this example: no matter what is changed, the line cannot go faster than Operation 5, so resources must be concentrated there to increase efficiency.

Operation 3 occurs simultaneously with Operation 2 but takes less than half the time of Operation 2. Therefore Operation 2 is critical and will remain so until it can be reduced to less than .33 min/part of the simultaneous operation. The same is true of Operation 6, which is simultaneous with Operation 5. Until Operation 5 takes less time than Operation 6, Operation 5 remains the critical path.

Most projects are much more complicated.

## Value Stream Mapping Diagrams

Value stream mapping looks at all the steps in a cycle, including the flow of information, and looks for waste. Waste costs money.

If waste is eliminated profitability increases. Value Stream Mapping includes the flow of information. There will be three parallel diagrams: the information flow, the process map, and the timeline.

The process flow is similar to the example above, which shows the steps in the process and the time associated with each step. The timeline is built from the data entered in the process flow. This includes time waiting for information such as a response from a customer or a testing facility.

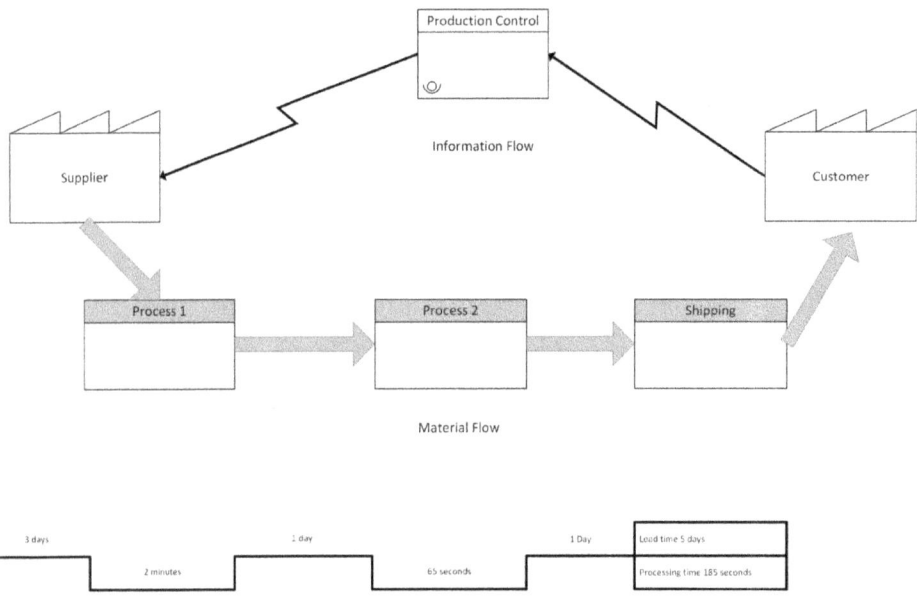

This tool can be used to identify the amount of time each step takes with the goal of reducing the throughput time, and includes the influence of waiting for information. [5]

## Total Productivity Maintenance

Total Productivity Maintenance (TPM) is attributed to a Toyota supplier. The idea is to increase overall equipment effectiveness (OEE), which is calculated by multiplying the run speed by the availability by the quality.

5 https://en.wikipedia.org/wiki/Value_stream_mapping

## Performance x Availability x Quality = OEE

Performance is the actual running speed minus stop times that are not due to breakdowns. Availability is the time minus breakdowns and changeovers. The quality is the non-conformances. This is compared to the actual available minutes of produc- 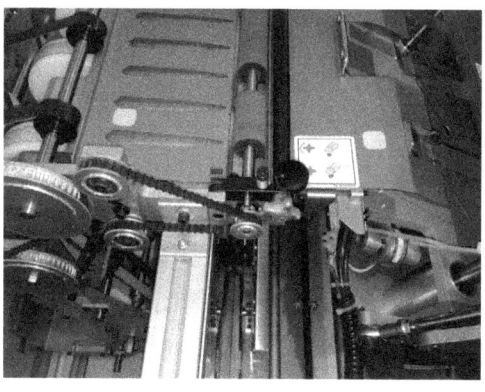 tion time. The objective is to eliminate breakdowns or machines running at less than optimum speed and of course non-conformances. This is an extremely effective tool in lowering costs and generally is accepted by a workforce who doesn't like breakdowns any more than management.

### Real life example

A company did a TPM project with a specific machine. There were three gauges on the machine which were critical for the operator to monitor. One gauge was on the opposite side of the operator station. The other two were on the same side as the station but located in difficult to spot locations. Each gauge was an arrow pointing to a range of numbers. One gauge needed to read approximately 3 on a clock face. The second gauge had to be at 12 on the clock, and the third gauge had to be at 9 on the clock. Several machine breakdowns and the production of non-conforming parts occurred because the operator misread or forgot to read one of the gauges. The project team moved the gauges to where they could be easily seen while standing at the operator station and replaced the gauges so the optimum position for all the needles was 12 on a clock. This eliminated the gauge error downtime and non-conforming product.

## Single Minute Exchange of Dies

Single Minute Exchange of Dies (SMED) focuses on reducing changeover times. The idea is to reduce changeovers to less than 10 minutes. This allows for faster response to customers and re-duced inventory holding costs, smaller lot sizes, and smoother start-ups. This is an excellent tool especially when used in con-junction with TPM.

### Real life example

Remember the example of the German plastic in-jection molding company? They were very specific in the configuration of the dies and the presses. Due to this consistency and optimization they could do a die change in 10 minutes with the same color plastic and 20 minutes with a color change. I recently had a plastic molding client who had to take 8 hours to do a color change. Think of the parts they could have made in that change-over time using a system like the German company.

Generally, a cross-functional team is needed to create the im-provement. Getting the right people on the team is critical, and having a facilitator who can lead without dominating is must. Make sure the people on the team have a vested interest in its success. Do not assume the manager of the area will support it because the productivity of the area will improve. The most fre-quent cause of failure of these types of projects is sabotage from managers afraid they will no longer be valued if problems go away.

## Summary:

- Continuous improvement is critical to the long-term profitability and even existence of a company.
- There are a number of tools which can be used.
- The focus of continuous improvement is fixing what isn't broken, not waiting for it to break and then applying the fix in other areas.
- Cross-functional teams are most effective but must have clear direction and goals.
- Drive out fear for people related to the project but not on the team, so they don't sabotage the team efforts. All people must know they are valued.

# The End

This little book was intended to help the small business owner to be successful at making a profit, staying in business, and providing a secure future for the owner and the employees. The intent was to give a broad overview so the owner could pursue those avenues and tools which work best for their company. No two companies are exactly the same; they are as unique as snowflakes. To keep from disappearing as quickly as a snowflake in the sun a company must always strive to improve. If Technacon Company Inc. can assist in that endeavor, please feel free to contact us via our website www.technacon.com or at technacon1986@sbcglobal.net.